Photo by Tom Soper

LISA THOMPSON

worked as a radio broadcast assistant first at the BBC and then for an independent production company making plays and comedy programmes. She grew up in Essex and now lives in Suffolk with her family.

The Goldfish Boy was one of the bestselling debuts of 2017 and was shortlisted for a number of prizes, including the Waterstones Children's Book Prize. Her stunning second book, *The Light Jar*, was chosen as the Children's Book of the Week in *The Times*, the *Guardian* and the *Observer* on publication, and *The Day I Was Erased* was Children's Book of the Week in *The Times*.

Other books by Lisa Thompson

FROM THE AUTHOR OF
THE GOLDFISH BOY

LISA THOMPSON

THE MYSTERY OF THE FOREVER WEEKEND

SCHOLASTIC

Published in the UK by Scholastic, 2024
1 London Bridge, London, SE1 9BG
Scholastic Ireland, 89E Lagan Road,
Dublin Industrial Estate, Glasnevin, Dublin, D11 HP5F

Text © Lisa Thompson, 2024
Illustrations © Gemma Correll, 2024

ISBN 978 0702 32264 8

A CIP catalogue record for this book
is available from the British Library.

Printed and bound in Great Britain by Clays Ltd, Elcograf S.p.A
Paper made from wood grown in sustainable forests
and other controlled sources.

1 3 5 7 9 10 8 6 4 2

www.scholastic.co.uk

For Amy B

CHAPTER ONE

There are three things about school that stress me out.

Number one is maths. I can't do it and most of it is pretty pointless anyway. For example: when will I ever need to work out the area of a triangle in real life? As far as I'm concerned, it's a complete waste of time. Maths lessons are the worst. Especially when our teacher, Mr Davy, fires mental arithmetic questions at us to keep our brains "maths fit". Last week we were all quietly working through a sheet of fractions when he suddenly shouted:

"Cory Turner! Seven minus five, plus eight and then multiplied by twelve. What's the answer?"

I looked up at him and my cheeks began to burn. What did he say? Seven minus five? Well, that was two. But then in my head all I could see was the number two surrounded by a jumble of other numbers fluttering around like butterflies. I couldn't get a hold of them to work out the next bit.

Mr Davy frowned. "Come on, Cory. You should be able to do this one. This is basic stuff."

I swallowed. Opened my mouth, closed it again, then opened it as I plucked a number from my brain. "Ninety-nine?" I said.

Mr Davy sighed. "Anyone else?" No one volunteered so he began to do the sum on the whiteboard while we watched. Then he turned and faced the class.

"You've got to practise your maths, 7A. As you know, it's the midterm maths exam soon. You're in the bottom set of your year. If you do badly in this exam then who knows where you'll end up. There is no bottom-bottom."

Someone snorted but Mr Davy just sighed again and looked incredibly disappointed.

The second thing that stresses me out is a daytime television game show called *Déjà Vu*. You're probably wondering why on earth a TV show has made my list. Let me explain.

"Déjà vu" is a French saying that means "already seen". You've probably experienced it before. There you are, pouring some cereal into a bowl for your breakfast and, for a split second, you feel like you've done it before. I don't mean you feel like you did it the day before – I mean it feels like you have lived the moment already. It's an actual, real-life phenomenon. People call it having "déjà vu" and that's what the TV game show is all about. On the show, the contestants watch a few seconds of film and then they watch the same piece again and decide if the second version is an exact copy of the first or if it's been changed. It's kind of like playing "spot the difference", I guess. And if it turns out that the clip is exactly the same the second time round, that's when the audience shout out:

"NOW *THAT'S* DÉJÀ VU!"

I hate that catchphrase. I hear it every single day as it's shouted at me in the school corridors, across the playground and in the canteen. And the reason it's shouted at me is because my dad is Dennis Turner, the presenter of *Déjà Vu*. Having a parent who's the presenter of a rubbish TV game show that barely anyone watches any more is no fun, I can tell you. It's embarrassing. Especially when I have to be seen in public with him…

*

I was lying on my bed with my maths book open, ready to do some revision for the looming exam. Our old Jack Russell, Bingo, was sound asleep on my bed. We'd rescued him five years ago. His previous owner had died, and she apparently used to play bingo a lot – that's how he got his name. He was quite old when he came to live with us and his reddish-brown fur has faded, as if he's been sitting in the sun for too long. You can see milky-coloured circles in his eyes in some lights, and Mum says that his sight isn't as good as it was. He never used to be allowed upstairs, but the older he becomes the more he gets away with – including sleeping on my bed.

Mum knocked on my door and walked in without waiting for an answer. I quickly turned my maths book over so that she couldn't see my crossings-out or the comments that Mr Davy had made in red pen.

"Hello, Mr Bingo," said Mum. Bingo rolled on to his back and she tickled his tummy.

"You'd better start getting ready, Cory," said Mum. "We've got to leave soon."

I frowned. We were going somewhere? Mum spotted my reaction.

"Dad's opening that new supermarket, remember?"

I groaned. I'd completely forgotten! Because he

was a TV "celebrity", Dad did stuff like this now and then so he could earn a bit of extra money. But I'm not sure where that extra money ended up. We still had lots of things at home that needed fixing including a washing machine that wouldn't spin and a car that dripped oil on to our driveway and made a loud popping noise whenever we went out in it. Fortunately, this time I was busy so they'd have to go without me.

"I can't come," I said. "I'm leaving in fifteen minutes."

Rowan was my best friend and his mum worked as a physiotherapist for our local football team. She got two free tickets for all their home games and Rowan always asked me to go with him. Boxwick Wanderers weren't the best, but this afternoon they were playing in the semi-final of a cup match.

Mum frowned. "You know how we support each other in this family, Cory, and Dad really wants us to be there. You did say you'd come."

She was right. I had. But I had also told Rowan I'd go to the match with him. And he really wouldn't be happy if I let him down this late in the day. He'd been a bit funny with me lately, as if I was getting on his nerves or something.

Mum was waiting for an answer.

"But it's the semi-final, Mum!"

"I'm sorry, Cory. I'm sure Rowan can find someone else to go with," said Mum. She checked her watch. "Right. You've got an hour. Have a shower and give your hair a brush. OK?"

I dropped my head on to my arm. Going to events with Dad was excruciating.

I picked up my phone. How was I going to tell Rowan? He had definitely been avoiding me at school lately. I'd also noticed that when anyone yelled "Now *that's* déjà vu!" at me, he'd laugh. He never used to do that.

I decided a little lie wouldn't hurt.

Hi Rowan. Can't make football. Feel sick.
Sorry. Cory.

Rowan immediately replied.

What?! But it's the CUP!

I sent back a sad face emoji.

I hated lying but I didn't want to draw attention to Dad's job any more than I had to. And I was sure that if I'd told him the truth – "Sorry but I've got to go and watch my dad make a fool of himself. Again." – he just wouldn't understand.

I looked in the mirror on my wardrobe door and scraped my fingers through my hair. My phone beeped.

Forget it. I'll ask Will. He won't let me down.

I sighed. And there we have it: the third thing on my list that makes me dread going to school each day.

A boy called Will Higgs.

CHAPTER TWO

Will Higgs isn't a bully. He doesn't get into trouble at school. I've never known him to be in detention or get a late mark or to backchat a teacher. He's a champion swimmer so he's always going up on stage in assembly to show off his medals or be presented with a certificate for the fastest race time in some district swimming event or something. And he's in all the top sets at school and everyone, including the teachers, really like him. But I know for a fact that Will Higgs doesn't like *me* one little bit. And I know he doesn't like me because he told me. To my face.

When we started at Boxwick Academy we tended to hang around with the kids we already knew from primary school. I had been best mates with Rowan since year two so we stuck together. But just a couple of weeks into the term I got paired up with Will in a science lesson. We'd not really spoken before, so I thought I'd better introduce myself as I sat down next to him

"Hi. I'm Cory," I said.

"I know who you are," said Will, not looking up from the instruction sheet he had in front of him. "You're the one with the *famous* dad."

I didn't really know what to make of that. Yes, Dad was famous, but I wished he wasn't. I wished he had a normal job and worked in a bank or a shop or something. And Will had said it in a nasty way. I decided it was probably best to ignore it. I looked down at the sheet our teacher had handed out. It listed the instructions to make invisible ink.

"Should I measure out the chemicals or do you want to?" I asked.

Will put on a pair of safety goggles.

"I'll do it, *obviously*," he said, making a start. I quickly put my goggles on too. I didn't understand why he was being so rude to me. What had I done? I thought we'd take turns to mix the solution, but Will just carried on as if I wasn't even there. Once the ink was made, we had to use a small paintbrush to write something on a piece of paper. I thought I'd get to do that at least, but Will grabbed the brush, dipped it into the solution and wrote something out. When he was finished, he sat back, folding his arms.

"You can do the next bit," he said.

I checked the instructions.

"Right, so next we need to wash the paint over the paper to read the message," I said.

Will grinned. "Go on then."

I dipped a bigger brush into some purple paint then swiped it across the paper. Will's words began to reveal themselves. I read them out loud.

"I DON'T LIKE YOU." I looked at Will. "Is this supposed to be a message for me?"

Will nodded. I was confused.

"But you don't even know me!" I said. "Why would you say that?"

Will picked up the piece of paper and screwed it up into a tight ball.

"I don't like you, Cory Turner. I never have and I never will."

I was gobsmacked. What had I done?

"But why?" I asked.

Will shrugged as if this feeling he had was completely out of his control and there was nothing that he could do about it. I was going to ask if I'd done something to upset him when our teacher started talking about the experiment. We sat in silence for the rest of the lesson, and when it was over he picked up his bag and left without even looking at me.

I told Rowan what had happened but he didn't get why I was so bothered about it.

"He was probably just winding you up. Will's like that. He's *well* funny! You just don't get his sense of humour."

But I didn't find him amusing. In fact, Will was the one who started the trend of shouting "Now *that's* déjà vu!" at me. I think most people would have lost interest after the first few times, but Will seemed determined to keep it going. After a few weeks I decided the best thing I could do was to stay out of his way. He clearly had an issue with me and I still hadn't found out what it was. Rowan, however, thought that Will was "brilliant" so it didn't surprise me that as soon as I said I couldn't go to the match, he invited him to take my place.

I got ready for the supermarket opening and went downstairs. Dad was in the hallway, checking his reflection in the wall mirror. He was wearing the outfit he wore when he presented *Déjà Vu*: a purple sparkly suit and a lemon-coloured shirt.

"Ready to go, Cory?" he said, smoothing down his eyebrows. I grunted.

Mum was scrolling on her phone, frowning.

"Debbie and Martin are off to New York next week," she said. "Debs said they're there for six months. Can you imagine? What an experience."

Dad paused for a moment, then went back to checking his reflection.

"Martin did tell me something about it."

Mum sighed and dropped her phone into her bag.

"It's a shame you gave up on acting, Dennis," she said. "You could be on Broadway now too. You've got the talent for it."

Dad ran his tongue over the front of his teeth.

"I didn't give up on acting, Jenna. I was getting typecast in that soap. You know I was. I had to quit."

I could feel an argument brewing. I put my trainers on and Bingo wandered over to me, thinking it must be walkies time. I stroked his soft ears and he blinked his cloudy brown eyes at me.

"Why don't you have a word with Martin? See if he can introduce you to a few directors?" said Mum. "You know I'll always support you. I just think there might be bigger, better things out there for you!"

"Oh, not this again, Jenna. I don't interfere in your job so why do you feel the need to interfere with mine?"

Mum folded her arms. "I'm not interfering. I care. And we need more money to pay the bills."

When they started talking about money I knew it was time to get out of the way.

"I'll wait outside," I mumbled, opening the front door.

This discussion was one I'd heard many times. Dad and Martin had been best friends when they studied acting back in their early twenties. Dad was the first of them to get a job – a part in a soap opera. But after a few years he told Mum he felt "trapped" and that he wanted to do theatre work. He quit around the time I was born and started presenting *Déjà Vu*. It was popular for a while but within a few years it ended up on a channel that barely anyone watched and Dad's salary was halved. To make things worse, his student friend, Martin, went on to make three Hollywood films and was inundated with job offers.

They came out of the house a few minutes later and I could tell by their folded arms that they were upset with each other. We got in the car, Mum and Dad both slamming their doors, and then Dad reversed off the driveway.

Our car was really embarrassing, and I hated going out in it. For a start it looked awful with flaking paint and rusty doors. But worse than that was the noise it made. Every few metres it let off a loud *POP* from its back end, making passers-by clutch their chests in shock. It was like some sort of clown's car. After the third *POP* I had to say something.

"Can't we get that noise fixed, Dad? It's going to give someone a heart attack."

Dad patted the steering wheel.

"Ah, it's not that bad!" he said, brightly. "Exhaust pipes don't come cheap you know."

"What about the money you get from *Déjà Vu*? Surely that can pay for it?" I said. I looked at Mum who was silent and just staring out of the window.

Dad indicated to turn left at a mini roundabout.

"Well, you know, it's not primetime TV or anything. And my agent takes a percentage because she's the person that gets me the work. There's not much left after the mortgage and the bills."

He also spent an awful lot of time at the hairdressers and at the dentist getting his teeth whitened. Then there was the gym, the personal trainer and the weekly manicures. He said he had to look his best for TV.

Mum also worked in the entertainment industry. She was a make-up artist, and she took jobs as and when she could get them. That's how she met Dad, in fact, on the set of *Albany Road*, the soap he used to work on.

I stared out of the window and wondered how Will and Rowan were getting on at the match. Will didn't even *like* football. Just last week he'd said that rugby was the only team sport worth watching and Rowan had nodded as if he agreed, even though I knew he loved football more than anything in the world.

Eventually we pulled up outside the brand-new supermarket that Dad was opening: Mega-Meals. Across the front of the wide glass doors was a red ribbon and standing to one side, presumably waiting for my dad to turn up, were six people. Five of them were wearing bottle-green polo tops with a "Mega-Meals" print that matched the shop's sign. In front of them was a man in a shirt, tie and trousers who I guessed must be the manager.

"Ah! There's the crowd!" said Dad. "Marvellous."

"It's just the people who work here, Dad," I grumbled. "No one has come. As usual."

Mum glanced round at me and glared. It was OK for her to moan at Dad but it seemed that I wasn't allowed to say anything. The man in the shirt and tie strode over and we all got out of the car.

"Dennis! You're here. Malcolm Spangle," said the man. They shook hands. "Right, let's get you into position, shall we? I'm afraid the local journalist hasn't been able to make it. He's only just left reporting on a football match which went to penalties." I groaned. I had probably missed the best match of the season for this!

I followed Mum and Dad towards the shop, then slunk off to one side and stood by a litter bin. Dad would be too busy being a "celebrity" to realize I was hiding. He shook all of the employees' hands and then an old woman with a walking frame approached and Dad gave her his best grin, holding out his arms.

"Why, hello!" he said. "Are you after an autograph?" Dad reached into his jacket pocket for the black and white portrait photos he always carried.

"No, I'm not," snapped the old woman. "Is this going to take all day? I need some bread."

Dad's smile faltered a little. He turned the manager.

"Let's get the show on the road, shall we, Malcolm?"

The supermarket manager nodded and cleared his throat. "Thank you all for coming to this very special day. I am delighted to welcome a veteran of popular entertainment. Presenter of TV game show *Déjà Vu* ... DENNIS TURNER!"

There was a smattering of applause from the employees and Mum, and then Dad stepped forward and waved his arms around as if he'd just walked out on to the stage at Wembley Stadium.

"Thank you! Thank you! Thank you very much, everyone!" he said. The clapping stopped abruptly. "Some people think that being a celebrity would mean that I'd lose touch with my community. Not true. There is nothing I like more about my job than the opportunities it gives me to celebrate momentous occasions, such as this one."

One of the employees sneezed into his hand then wiped it on his trousers.

"I remember when I was a child I—"

"Oh, get on with it, would you?" cried the old woman.

Dad closed his mouth and then opened it to carry on, but Malcolm thrust a pair of silver scissors into Dad's hands. Dad stepped closer to the ribbon.

"It gives me great pleasure in declaring this Mega-Meal's branch officially … OPEN!"

Dad snipped the ribbon and Mum and the staff gave another ripple of applause. The old woman hurried forward, pushing Dad out of the way to go inside. Malcolm took the scissors from Dad and passed him a ten pound note which Dad folded and put in his pocket. I thought that was a bit strange. Surely he'd have been paid more than £10? OK, so he wasn't mega famous, but he was quite well known. Just then a voice shouted loudly behind me.

"Now *that's* déjà vu!"

I span round and my stomach plummeted. It was Will and Rowan. They must be on their way home from the match. Dad heard his catchphrase being shouted out and he looked over and waved. Will waved back. A big grin on his face.

I wanted to run to the car, but they were walking over towards me. Rowan was holding a bag of doughnuts – something we usually shared on match days. He didn't look very happy.

"I thought you were sick?" he said, tilting his head on one side.

"I, erm, I felt a bit better. And Dad asked if I could come and see—"

"What sort of money does your dad get for gigs like this, then?" interrupted Will. "Is it like a grand or something? Two grand? Three?"

Rowan held the bag towards Will and he took a sugary doughnut and stuffed it into his mouth, licking at his fingers.

"I don't know," I said. "He has an agent who takes care of that."

Will was frowning – I hoped he wasn't thinking of any more questions.

"What happened at the football?" I asked Rowan.

Rowan's face brightened. "We won on penalties! It was amazing! You should have seen Stamford's save."

"Oh, that's brilliant!" I said. Rowan seemed to have forgiven me. For a moment at least. But then Will butted in.

"Shame you missed it really," said Will. "By the way, I've always wondered. Does your dad use a sunbed or is that a spray tan?" I looked over at Dad and realized what a strange colour his face was. He was talking to a woman with a buggy who had clearly just come to the supermarket to shop, not chat to an orange TV presenter.

"Um. I don't know," I said. Mum put her hand on Dad's arm and they began to walk towards us.

"Looks like we're going now," I said to Will, hoping that would make him leave, but he still had more to say. "Does someone make him dye his hair that colour or is it his choice? Is it in his contract or something?"

Will glanced at Rowan and they both began to snigger. Will wasn't even putting on his nice act and Rowan was still laughing! Why wasn't he sticking up for me? Mum and Dad joined us.

"Hello, Rowan!" said Mum. "How are you doing? Are your family well?"

"Yes, they're all fine, thank you," said Rowan.

Dad was grinning and I wished he'd shut his mouth. His teeth looked ridiculous. He looked at Will and then at me, waiting for me to introduce him.

"Oh. This is Will," I said.

Will held out his hand towards Dad who looked thrilled.

"Nice to meet you, Mr Turner," said Will. "I absolutely *love* your TV show. We watch it *all* the time."

"Oh, that's so nice!" said Dad, oblivious to Will's sarcasm. "Would you like a signed photo?"

He began to reach into his inside pocket when I shouted out, "NO!"

Everyone turned to look at me.

"We've got to go. I've got loads of revision, Mum, remember?" I grabbed Mum's wrist and pulled her a little. She frowned at me at first, but she understood how awkward this was for me.

"Yes, we'd better get going, Dennis," she said.

"Another time then," said Dad.

"Now *that's* déjà vu!" said Will, pointing a finger at Dad and giving him a wink.

Dad laughed and clapped his hands together.

"Fantastic!" he said.

I hurried them away and we got in the car.

As we pulled away the exhaust did another loud *POP*. I looked into the wing mirror and watched as Will pointed at our car and they both collapsed into hysterical laughter.

CHAPTER THREE

"Here he comes! The son of a celeb!"

"Now *that's* déjà vu!"

"I hear they needed crowd control at Mega-Meals on Sunday afternoon to keep the Dennis Turner fans at bay. Is that right, Cory?"

"I bet your dad would go to the opening of a bag of crisps!"

"Does your dad realize he looks like a Wotsit with teeth?"

As I walked along the school corridor, I deflected the barrage of Monday morning taunts in my usual way. They seemed to be getting meaner and I suspected that was down to Will stirring things up behind the scenes. I smiled and rolled my eyes and let out the occasional guffaw as I walked. In the past I'd tried to answer back, to correct their nasty comments or point out how wrong they were. But it didn't work. The only thing that made it slightly bearable was to pretend that I was in on the joke – that I was one of them and happy to laugh along about my dad's ridiculous job and how embarrassing he was. And let's face it, most of it was true. He *was* embarrassing.

I got to my form class and sat down next to Rowan. I hadn't heard from him since seeing him at Mega-Meals on Sunday.

"All right?" I said. I put my backpack under the desk. Rowan didn't say anything and just nodded at me.

"I'm sorry about missing the match. Mum and Dad wanted me to go to that supermarket opening thing and I…"

"Forget it," he interrupted.

I wanted to explain why I'd lied but our form tutor, Ms Horne, started talking.

"As I'm sure most of you know, this Saturday is the annual Ivy Hill fireworks display. What you may not know is the background story behind this local tradition which takes place in Boxwick each year. I'm pleased to say that the local library has curated an exhibition about this time-honoured event. Ms Horne pulled one of her serious-looking faces. You are lucky to live in a town that is rich with history. I urge you to go and take a look."

I mouthed "boring" at Rowan, but he didn't laugh. Ms Horne started a discussion about the news topics of the day, and it wasn't long before the bell went, signalling the end of form. Rowan stood up and put his bag on his shoulder. Then he turned to me.

"Are you coming to the match on Sunday then or what?"

"Of course I'm coming! I'm not going to miss the final, am I?" I said.

Rowan shrugged and I suddenly wondered if he would prefer to go with Will. Maybe they'd had such a good time that he was going to end up taking my ticket for every home match.

"See you at the gates later?" I said. We always met at the gates at the end of school, but Rowan walked off without saying anything.

I got my bag and felt a surge of dread in my guts. Not only was I rapidly losing my best friend, but I now had to face the worst lesson in the world: maths. I began a slow walk to my classroom. When I got there, Mr Davy was standing at the front, grinning at me. I braced myself.

"Oh … hang on a minute. Haven't you been in my lesson before?" he said.

I stood there, smiling feebly, and waited for him to continue. Mr Davy did this little routine most Monday mornings.

"It's very odd because I think…" He began to snigger. "I think I've seen you before." He screwed up his face and tapped his finger on his lips as if he was trying to place me. His acting was atrocious. Eventually his eyes widened, and he gasped.

"Now *that's* déjà vu!" he said, his shoulders shaking with laughter.

Yep. Even the teachers thought it was funny.

"Good one, sir," I muttered. I went to my desk and sank into my chair which was next to a girl called Agatha. We'd been sitting together in maths since we started high school but had never really spoken. She was in a few of my other classes and whenever I saw her she always looked thoroughly miserable. She was half slumped on the desk, her chin in her hand as she waited for the lesson to begin. Her brown hair was tied back into a low ponytail, and she was twiddling the ends around her finger.

Mr Davy walked around the class handing out worksheets. When he passed me, he gave me a pat on my shoulder as if he wanted to thank me for letting him do his little joke. Even though he taught the worst subject in school *and* he laughed about Dad's game show, he was all right really.

I was just getting my pencil case out of my bag when Agatha suddenly spoke.

"That must really get on your nerves. You know. The whole 'déjà vu' stuff."

"Yeah, you could say that," I said.

I took my pen out of my pencil case and hoped that we were going over statistics that we'd been learning in our last lesson. I'd not understood any of it and Mr Davy said we *had* to know it because it was going to be covered in the exam next week. We'd been told so many times that doing well in this exam was CRUCIAL and that it was VITAL that we did our best. The more Mr Davy went on about it, the more stressed I became and the harder it was to understand any of it.

"It's not even funny though, is it?" said Agatha. At first I thought she was talking about maths but then I realized she was still talking about *Déjà Vu*. "I've never seen it but it's not like you were a contestant or something. Your dad is the presenter. It's not really got anything to do with you." I'd never heard her say so much in one go.

"I guess," I said.

I picked up the sheet that Mr Davy had handed out. It looked like we were moving on to algebra. I chewed on my bottom lip. I suddenly felt a bit overwhelmed. My best friend was barely talking to me and now I had to do stupid maths. I was in danger of crying, and crying in class was literally the worst thing you could ever do. It happened once to a kid called Douglas in my French class. We'd been learning the words for various animals and when we got to *le lapin* he started bawling. *Le lapin* is French for rabbit, and it turned out his pet rabbit had died that weekend. Even though it was sad he didn't get any sympathy. For a while people forgot to yell "Now *that's* déjà vu!" at me and began shouting "Don't cry *le lapin*!" at Douglas instead.

I took a deep breath.

"Cory? Are you OK?" said Agatha.

I blinked and one of the tears accidentally escaped. I quickly blotted it with my sleeve and kept my face forwards.

"Yes," I snapped. "Of course I am." Mr Davy was writing a calculation on the whiteboard which included a bunch of numbers *and* letters.

I swallowed and turned my chair very slightly away from her so that she couldn't see me.

"OK, class. Let's get started, shall we? Right. Who wants to have a go at working out what 'c' means on this equation here? Anyone?"

The school day seemed to go on for ever but eventually the final bell went and I headed to the school gates to meet Rowan. As if the day couldn't get any worse, I spotted Will walking towards me. He was with Henry and Ellie who were part of the cool group.

"Well, would you look at that. It's Cory Turner again! Now *that's* déjà vu!" said Will.

I stared over his shoulder to see if I could spot Rowan.

"You do know I'm joking when I say stuff, don't you, Cory?" said Will. He stood right in front of me, his bright blue eyes twinkling in the sun.

"Sure," I said, trying to look around again.

"Hey. Why don't you come to Jaspers with us? We're going there now," said Will. Jaspers was an ice-cream parlour in town and a popular hangout after school. I'd been a couple of times with Rowan, but it was always full of kids from school yelling Dad's catchphrase at me.

"No thanks," I said. "I'm waiting for Rowan."

Will frowned. "You can't be. Rowan's nearly there already. He's grabbing a booth. Didn't he tell you?"

"Oh yeah," I lied. "I forgot." My mind was racing. Why hadn't Rowan told me that we weren't meeting like we usually did?

"Are you coming then or what?" said Ellie.

I didn't want to go, but if Rowan was there then maybe I should? I didn't want to end up with no friends at all.

"Sure," I said.

Will slapped me on the shoulder.

"Great! You can tell us all about what it's like to live with a Z … I mean A-list celebrity."

The three of them laughed and I felt a tightness beginning to grip my stomach. I wasn't sure if this was going to be a good idea, after all.

CHAPTER FOUR

When we got to Jaspers, Rowan was already there, sitting in one of the bright-red padded booths. When he saw me walking behind Will I noticed his smile drop.

"I didn't know *you* were coming too?" he mumbled.

"I didn't know *you* were," I fired back. Will sat beside Rowan and I sat on the other side of the table. Henry told me to move up and then he and Ellie squashed in next to me. It was only supposed to be a table for four. A woman wearing a pink and white striped shirt and dungarees came over.

"What can I get y'all," she said in a terrible American accent.

Everyone ordered ice creams but I didn't think I could stomach one, so I asked for a lemonade. When the woman left, Will leaned towards me.

"It's an ice cream parlour, Cory. You're supposed to eat ice cream." His grin was wide and he punched the top of my arm in an "only joking" way.

"Actually, I'm quite thirsty," I said. Which just sounded pathetic.

They all started talking about something that had happened in Henry's geography class and I took the chance to get my phone out to text Mum and Dad to let them know I'd be late. I'd just began to type …

Going to be l8

… when Will snatched the phone out of my hand.

"Hey! Give it back!" I said. I tried to grab it, but Will twisted round so he was facing the other way.

"Let's see what messages look like from a celebrity, shall we?" said Will.

"That's my phone!" I said. "It's private!" My mind raced as I tried to remember what messages were on there.

"Come on, Cory. Lighten up, eh? We're only having a bit of fun," said Will.

I looked at the others. Were they having fun?

Henry and Ellie were grinning. Rowan was smiling too, but I had known him long enough to see that he was feeling quite uncomfortable.

"Maybe you should give it back to him, Will," he mumbled. Will ignored him.

"Show us! What do they say?" said Ellie, sitting forward on the bench.

"There are photos! Oh, this is priceless," said Will.

I remembered some photos that Dad had sent when he'd been shopping. I felt sick.

Will slowly turned around with the phone facing outwards. On the screen was a picture that Dad had taken of his reflection in a changing room mirror. He was wearing a red sparkly suit and posing. Everyone collapsed into laughter.

"Listen to what he said!" Will read out my dad's text. "Makes me look younger, don't you think, Cory?"

"Younger?! He looks like a sweet wrapper!" said Ellie. And there was more agony to come.

"And Cory replied! 'Looks great, Dad!'"

I hadn't really meant it, but what else could I have said?

"How kind of you to lie to him like that," said Will. "Although you're quite good at lying, aren't you? Like when you told Rowan you felt sick on Sunday and couldn't go to the match."

Will winked, and then the waitress appeared with our order. While he was distracted with his ice cream, I took the chance to reach over and grab my phone back.

"It's all cool, Cory," said Will after the waitress left. "I think it's very sweet of you to support your dad like that. I'd be the same if my dad's career was failing. It's all about family, after all, isn't it?"

Everyone around the table nodded.

"It's like my swimming," continued Will. "My dad has to drive me to the pool every morning for training and then get the train to work. But he said he's making these sacrifices so that I can reach my true potential."

I wanted to vomit. I looked at the others to see if they could see through Will like I could, but they were all nodding in agreement.

"Are you going to the Ivy Hill fireworks on Saturday?" Rowan said suddenly. I kept my head down and sipped my drink.

"Yeah. We go every year," said Ellie. "My mum said it's important to support the town traditions or they'll die out."

"I don't get it," said Henry. "It's not New Year or

bonfire night. Why do we have fireworks now?"

Will scraped his spoon around the tall, glass dish. "It's for that kid, Ivy. She saved the town from burning down like hundreds of years ago or something."

"What did she do?" said Henry.

While they were talking, I quickly finished my text to Mum and Dad. I knew they'd start to worry if they hadn't heard from me soon. Dad replied straight away.

Have fun, kiddo! There's a surprise waiting
for you when you get home! :)

I had no idea what that was.

I decided I'd stayed long enough so I quickly slurped down the rest of my lemonade and put some coins on the table to pay for my drink.

"I've got to go," I mumbled. Henry and Ellie got up so I could get out.

"See ya, celeb-boy," said Will. He reached over and patted me on the shoulder. I shrugged him off and walked away.

When I got out into the fresh air, I breathed a huge sigh of relief. I didn't want to end up with no friends, but was being friends with them any better?

I wasn't sure.

I began to walk home and wondered what Dad's surprise could be. Dad's surprises were usually a bit naff, but maybe this time it was something good. Maybe he'd had an acting audition but not told us about it just in case we got our hopes up. Yes – I could imagine Dad doing something like that. And maybe his agent had just phoned to say he'd got the job – a major part in a big Hollywood movie! That could easily be it. Then I could go into school tomorrow and casually drop it into conversation that my dad wasn't a naff celebrity. He was, in fact, a talented actor who was in huge demand.

That would shut Will up.

CHAPTER FIVE

When I got home I pushed on the front door, but there was something blocking the way. I gave the door a big shove and managed to squeeze in.

"You're here!" said Dad, appearing in the hallway. He was wearing a dark pink jumper with "SUPERSTAR" written on the front in bold white writing. To me it felt like the more he was becoming a fading celebrity, the more he tried to stand out from the crowd. I wished he wouldn't.

"I bet you're wondering what the surprise is, aren't you?" said Dad.

I already had the feeling that Hollywood wasn't calling after all. And I was right. Dad jumped to one side and waved his hand at two piles of cardboard boxes that were blocking the door.

"Ta-da!" said Dad.

Each of the boxes was stamped with a logo that read:

STARLIGHT TOOTHPASTE!
For a smile as bright as the stars!

"Toothpaste?" I said. "Is that the surprise?"

A box on the top of one of the piles was open and Dad took out a tube and held it up to his face.

"Hello! I'm Dennis Turner. And I use Starlight toothpaste so that my smile is as bright as the stars!"

For a moment I thought he might have been having some kind of nervous breakdown.

"Did you order this much by mistake?"

Dad rolled his eyes and grinned. "Of course not. Don't you remember my TV advert? It premieres this evening on telly!"

"Oh," I said. I remembered a few months back Dad had gone to London for some filming. He'd been excited about it as he'd not done an advert before.

"And they've sent you some free toothpaste to say thank you. That's cool," I said, picking up a tube and taking a closer look. But when I looked back at Dad I noticed his smile had gone.

"Well, not exactly, Cory. Nothing in life is free, as they say!"

I looked at the boxes lining our hallway.

"You bought all of this?" I said.

Dad chuckled. "No! This is my payment! For the advert!"

I dropped the tube back in the box.

"They paid you ... in *toothpaste*?"

Dad raised his eyebrows and nodded. "Yes. Cool, eh? We'll have enough toothpaste to last us for years!"

"But we can't pay for things with toothpaste, Dad. What about the car? Couldn't you have been paid properly so we could get that noise fixed?"

Dad smiled but I couldn't see what was so funny. "Cory, some people don't have a car. You should be grateful we have one at all! Right, I'm going to make a cuppa. I'll give you a shout later when it's on!"

He headed off to the kitchen and I stared at the cardboard boxes. I wasn't ungrateful. I knew that we were lucky with what we had, but there were things to pay for. We had a leak in the ceiling in our bathroom and once I'd overheard Mum on the phone to my grandparents and she was clearly asking for help to pay our electricity and gas bills. What was Dad doing agreeing to be paid in toothpaste? And what was his agent doing by letting him agree?!

Just then Mum came down the stairs. My heart plummeted when I saw that she was carrying two heavy-looking cases. What was going on? Was she leaving? Mum and Dad had been arguing a lot lately. Had it got that bad?

"Hi, Cory," she said, grimly. She nodded her head towards the boxes. "You've seen them then?"

Suddenly the boxes of toothpaste didn't seem to matter any more.

"Where are you going, Mum?" I said, trying to disguise the panic in my voice.

I helped Mum as she struggled to the bottom step and we both dropped each case with a huff.

"Oh, I've got a last-minute job. One of the make-up artists on a shoot in Madrid has broken his wrist so I'm going over to help. It's all a bit rushed. I'm off to the airport now. The taxi should be here soon."

I realized then that one of the cases was full of the bits she'd need for her work.

"Oh, that's great!" I said, almost laughing with relief. "When will you be back?"

Mum put a small bag across her shoulder.

"I'm there for a week, so next Monday. You'll have

to cheer Dad on at the awards ceremony on your own on Sunday, I'm afraid.

I had no idea what awards she was talking about but suspected I had been told about it and hadn't really listened, so I didn't ask. She squeezed my shoulder and I saw her eyes fall on the toothpaste behind me. She pressed her lips together and shook her head slightly. Then she turned to put her jacket on. I really wished she wasn't going away.

I quickly raised a smile as she pulled me into a big hug.

A taxi beeped outside and she let go and kissed me on top of my head.

"I'm sure the week will fly by," she said.

Dad appeared from the kitchen.

"Oh, are you off, love?" he said.

"Yes, Dennis. Let me know how the advert goes." Mum put her arms around him and kissed him on the cheek, but I noticed she didn't hug him for as long as she usually did. "I'll text you when I get there."

She picked up her cases and squeezed around the boxes of toothpaste and out of the house.

Dad headed back to the kitchen and I stood in the hallway and stared at our front door. I suddenly had a strong urge to tell Mum not to go. Maybe it was because I was so bottled up with worry, but every fibre in my being was screaming at me to tell her to stay at home. I pushed past the boxes down the hall and flung the door open, but I was too late. The space outside our house was empty. The taxi had already gone.

CHAPTER SIX

"CORY? IT'S NEARLY ON! COME ON! YOU WON'T WANT TO MISS IT!"

I was lying on my bed, surrounded by maths books. I sighed and glanced at the time on my phone. It was quarter past seven. At least watching Dad's advert meant I didn't have to pretend to be doing any revision.

I made my way downstairs. Bingo was snoozing with his head hanging off the edge of the sofa and I lifted him up and shifted him so that he was a bit more comfortable. I slumped down beside him. Dad turned the TV on and began to flick through the channels.

"Right. Here we go," he said, stopping on an advert for washing-up liquid. "It shouldn't be long."

He sat down next to me and checked his watch

before staring back at the TV. The advert was promising that the washing-up liquid would give endless "suds and sparkles". When that one finished, an advert for a sports car began. The camera zoomed in on a beautiful silver car, speeding through country lanes, surrounded by lush green fields and a clear blue sky.

Dad checked his watch yet again.

"I reckon it'll be on after this one," he said. His knees jiggled up and down as he bit on his bottom lip.

The sports car advert cut to the driver who had his arm resting on the open window as he drove. I vaguely recognized him.

"That's Timothy Gosling!" said Dad. "He presents *Your Cash, My Cash*."

The advert was incredibly slick with dramatic music. Timothy was smiling as if he was having the best day of his life. The camera pulled back and up for an aerial shot of the car winding its way along the lanes. There was a particularly sharp bend and then the car turned into a driveway, speeding up the gravel path and skidding to a stop outside a beautiful white mansion.

"You wouldn't want to drive on gravel like that in real life," said Dad. "Those stones could chip a window."

The voiceover boomed: *"Your drive home will never be the same again."*

Timothy got out of the car, slammed the door, and tossed the key into the air, catching it in one hand. He stared right at the camera and his eye did an actual twinkle. I wondered if that was one of his acting skills, like being able to speak another language or ride a horse. For Timothy it would be can-make-eyes-twinkle-on-demand.

The screen then turned black and the car's brand name faded into focus.

Dad's face filled the TV screen. He sprang forward, making me jump.

"It's on!" he gasped. He was wearing a sparkly suit like the ones he wore on *Déjà Vu* and he was standing in front of a giant model of a tooth that was dangling on some string. He held a tube of toothpaste right next to his face.

"Hello. I'm Dennis Turner. And I use Starlight toothpaste so that my smile is as bright as the stars!"

The screen cut away to Dad in a very posh-looking bathroom wearing some blue and white striped pyjamas. He was looking at himself in a mirror while brushing his teeth. Dad's voice-over told us how Starlight toothpaste not only tackled plaque but gently cleaned enamel and reduced stains. The advert cut back to Dad standing in his suit with the massive tooth behind him.

"Choose Starlight toothpaste for your very own ... showbiz smile!" said Dad. And then he grinned. The camera zoomed in on Dad's unnaturally white teeth and there was a little sparkle on Dad's incisor. Unlike Timothy's twinkling eye though, this was clearly made by a special effect. The screen faded and another advert came on.

"Boom!" said Dad, grinning from ear to ear. "Well, I'm really pleased with that. What do you think, Cory? Are you proud of your dad's first advert?"

It was pretty rubbish, but at the end of the day it could have been much worse. And if you blinked for long enough you might miss it. I hoped no one at school had seen it. Especially Will.

"It was all right," I said.

"Yes. I'm pleased with that," said Dad. "I wonder if Sydney has seen it."

He got his phone out of his pocket and wandered out of the room as he began to text.

My own phone buzzed in my pocket. It was a notification for a school group chat which I rarely used.

Did you just see Cory's dad's advert for
toothpaste?

I thought his dad had his teeth
professionally whitened!

It's not the toothpaste making them look like
that then?

I sat there, horrified, as I watched the flurry of
messages appearing one after the other. Had they
forgotten that I was on the chat and could read
everything they were saying? I was just wondering if
I should type something when Will joined in.

I'm not being mean or anything, but aren't
"celebs" supposed to be rich? Have you
seen their car?! It should be in a scrapyard!

A few people began agreeing with Will, one of them
commenting on my cheap trainers and then Rowan
sent a laughing emoji. I felt sick. How could he join
in like that and not stick up for me?

"This is so unfair," I said, thumping my hand
on the sofa.

Bingo raised his head and looked up at me and I stroked his warm back. He settled back down and his chest rose and fell with each snore. It must be so simple being a dog and not having any worries.

Later that evening at dinner I pushed my food around my plate while Dad went on and on about his advert.

"Starlight toothpaste could bring in more work, Cory. Who knows what I'll be advertising next! Designer aftershave? A luxury cruise? It could lead to some really big things!"

I scooped some mashed potato on to my fork, then scraped it off again. I wasn't very hungry. The messages on the group chat had really churned my stomach.

"Is there any chance that someone will pay you in actual money next time?" I blurted out.

Dad frowned as he chewed his food. "You have to remember that this is a competitive business, Cory. There are hundreds if not thousands of 'Dennis Turners' out there, trying to get a bite of the celebrity apple!"

I dropped my fork and it clattered on to my plate.

"More Dennis Turners?! I doubt it, Dad. Who would want to be you?"

Dad looked at me, hurt and confused. I pressed my lips together.

We ate in silence for a while.

"Is everything OK, Cory?" said Dad. "Have you got something on your mind? You can tell me, you know."

I took a deep breath. There was a lot on my mind. Getting through the next four days at school was one of them. And worrying about Mum and Dad and if they were going to split up. And the maths test next week. And losing my best friend to that idiot Will. Maybe it would be better for me to talk about it? Maybe Dad could help? I put my knife and fork on the side of my plate. Dad was waiting for me to say something but then his phone lit up.

"It's from my agent, Sydney! She said she saw the advert and she thought it was adequate." He frowned. "Adequate? I wonder what she meant by adequate."

I pushed my chair back as I stood up.

Dad was still staring at his phone, deep in thought. "She means good, doesn't she? Or great? I think she means great. What do you think, Cory?"

I sighed. "I don't know, Dad," I said. "I'm going to bed. I'm tired."

*

After my bath I put on my pyjamas. Then I packed my backpack for school and got my uniform ready, draping it over my chair. If I got my things ready the night before it meant another ten minutes in bed.

That night, I dreamt I turned up at school and there was no one there. I walked around the perimeter of the playground, then checked the hall and my form room. The place was utterly deserted. The silence was really eerie. I made my way down the corridor to the main doors when I heard a noise behind me. I slowly turned. Heading towards me was a giant white tooth hovering just above the ground. It was just like the one in Dad's advert! I walked away, but when I looked back the tooth was gaining on me. I began to run but it was no good, the corridor was going on and on and didn't seem to have an end. And the tooth was getting closer and closer. I began to call out, "Dad! Mum! Help me!" but it was no good. It was about to press into my back but then I stumbled and jolted awake. I lay sweating underneath my duvet, my heart pounding. I checked my clock and groaned when I saw there were two hours to go until I had to get up for school.

I rolled over and closed my eyes, even though the chance of getting back to sleep now was pretty much zero.

CHAPTER SEVEN

The week dragged on and on. Not only had I had to ignore the usual shouts of "Now *that's* déjà vu" in the corridor, I also had to put up with a new wisecrack – people shielding their eyes and crying, "Whoa, Cory! Your smile is as bright as the stars!" at me.

Hilarious.

And, as always, Will was the one laughing the loudest while telling me it was all "just a joke". But now, *finally*, it was Friday and I had two glorious days of NO SCHOOL ahead of me. I was still worried about the maths exam that was looming on Monday, and the fact that Rowan was clearly avoiding me. I asked him if he wanted to go for a kick about on the field after school, but he said he was busy. While I was out walking Bingo I spotted Rowan "busy" with Will as they queued up at the fish and chips shop. They didn't see me and I decided not to go up to them and say anything or I'd look really sad and bitter. Besides, the Ivy Hill fireworks were tomorrow so I would see Rowan there and I'd bring up the match on Sunday. If there was anything that was going to sort our friendship out it was football. And everyone loved the fireworks so he was bound to be in a good mood from the start.

My first memory of the Ivy Hill fireworks was when I was five years old. Mum had buttoned up my coat and put a woolly hat on my head, even though it wasn't exactly cold.

"Will the fireworks go 'bang'?" I asked.

"Some of them will," said Dad. "But we can do this if it's too loud." He put his hands over his ears and pulled a face and I giggled. I remember thinking Dad was hilarious. Everything he did seemed to be the funniest thing I'd ever seen. It was only in the last few years since his career took a nosedive and he began acting like a fool that he became embarrassing rather than entertaining.

There was a crowd of people heading to Ivy Hill and I walked between Mum and Dad and held on to their hands. Things were different back then. *Déjà Vu* was a popular game show on a popular channel and as we walked lots of people called out to Dad.

"Hey, Dennis! Good to see you!"

"Oh look! It's Dennis Turner! Can I have your autograph?"

"Dennis, can me and the wife have a selfie?"

Because everyone kept talking to Dad it took us a while to reach the top of the hill. There was the smell of popcorn and frying onions in the air.

"Who wants a hot dog?" said Dad.

"Me!" I said. The evening was just getting better and better! Not only was I allowed to stay up late but I was getting more food! Dad made his way through the crowd to the hot-dog stand.

"Mummy? Can you tell me about Ivy again?" I asked.

"You'll be able to tell me the story yourself before long!" said Mum.

"Please?"

"OK," said Mum, smiling. "A long, long time ago, back in the eighteen hundreds, most of Boxwick was fields and farmhouses. There were no cars or roads, no school or library. None of these big buildings existed."

Mum was quiet for a moment as we looked down on to the town from Ivy Hill. The windows of the houses were dotted with dim lights and there was a white glow on the roads from the car headlamps.

"Where did Ivy live?" I asked Mum. She crouched down beside me and pointed towards the church. Its tall spire was lit up with a warm yellow light.

"Her house was just over that way," she said. "But it's long gone now."

I blinked towards the church, imagining a little thatched cottage nestled to the side.

"One day," continued Mum, "Ivy was playing outside while her mother peeled vegetables. There was a little apple tree in their garden and Ivy climbed to the top. When she was up high, she could smell something in the air. Smoke! It had been a hot and dry summer and one of the fields was burning! She hurried back down and ran inside to tell her mum. If the crops were on fire their houses were at risk!"

I gasped and put my hand to my mouth, even though I knew what was going to happen.

Mum carried on. "Ivy and her mum ran from house to house calling out 'FIRE! FIRE!' There weren't any fire engines back then so the villagers rushed out of their homes carrying buckets and pans and ran to the well, filling them with water. They tried to put the fire out, but it was no good. The fire was getting bigger."

I slipped my hand into Mum's and she gave it a little squeeze.

"As the grown-ups carried on, trying desperately to put out the flames, Ivy saw that the fire was now in every direction. They were surrounded. One of the farmers began to shout, 'Get to the hill! Get to the hill!'"

I looked at the crowds around me, imagining they were all villagers from the eighteen hundreds. It must have been scary.

"The villagers stood right here on this hill and watched in silence as the fire spread dangerously close to their homes. There was nothing anyone could do."

Mum shook her head.

"And then what happened?" My stomach tingled. The next part of the story was my favourite bit.

"Well, then something quite magical happened," said Mum. "As they stood there in silence, watching their village being slowly destroyed, Ivy took a step forward. She held out her arms and began to chant: *'I wish the fire would go away! I wish the fire would go away!'*"

"I wish the fire would go away!" I copied. Mum grinned at me.

"Over and over she said those same words; I wish

the fire would go away," said Mum. "And then, one of the farmers shouted, 'Look! The fire is dying out!'"

I clapped my hands together.

"The villagers couldn't believe it! As they watched, the fire began to splutter and spit before completely fizzling out. There was no explanation for it. But from that day on this hill has always been known as Ivy Hill, and every year there has been a celebration to say thank you to that little girl who saved the town and who was very, very brave indeed."

"And what about the wishes?" I said. "Tell me about the wishes!"

Mum picked me up and I wrapped my arms around her neck.

"The saying goes that Ivy Hill has magical powers," said Mum. "If you stand on the top and whisper your wish into the night sky, just like Ivy did that day, your wish might come true."

She smiled and pressed her forehead against mine.

"I wish the fireworks would start," I whispered. Just then there was a loud *WHOOSH* and a huge rocket exploded into the sky right above our heads. We both gasped and Mum's eyes widened as she began to laugh. I giggled and watched the firework's sparkles reflected in her eyes.

CHAPTER EIGHT

I spent Saturday morning lying in bed and thinking about doing some maths revision but not actually doing any. I was scrolling through my phone when Dad knocked and asked if I fancied going into town to do some shopping.

"We can go and get some cake somewhere too if you like?"

I knew he was just making an effort as Mum was away. We never did things like this usually.

"Can't. I've got loads of homework," I said. I also didn't want to be seen out in public with Dad unless I really had to. We might bump into someone we knew and that would just make the teasing worse.

"OK," said Dad, sounding a little deflated. "Well, we've got the fireworks tonight. That'll be fun!"

"Yep," I said, still staring at my phone. I was planning to distance myself and find Rowan as soon as we got there.

I hoped Dad would leave, but he saw Bingo curled up at the end of my bed, sound asleep. "There he is! Mr Bingo himself!" He then cleared his throat and began to speak like a bingo caller.

"Kelly's eye ... number one! Rise and shine ... twenty-nine!"

I groaned inwardly. In a game of bingo you're given a piece of card with random numbers on it. The bingo caller reads out numbers and you cross them off when you get a match. When you've crossed off all the numbers on your card you shout out "BINGO!" and for some reason, bingo callers make funny comments when they say the numbers. It's like an old tradition or something. Because we have a dog called Bingo, Dad being Dad likes to call out the phrases, thinking he's funny. Bingo began to wag his tail as Dad got louder and louder.

"Unlucky for some ... thirteen! Two little ducks ... twenty-two!"

I didn't react. If Dad thought I was finding this in the slightest bit entertaining then he'd never stop. And there were a lot of numbers to get through. He stood there for a bit, then patted Bingo on the head.

"Right. I'm off then. I'll see you later."

"OK. Bye," I said. I had managed a whole conversation without looking at him.

As soon as I heard the front door close I hauled myself out of bed and headed downstairs in my pyjamas. I made a sandwich for lunch then flopped on to the sofa and scrolled through the TV channels. I saw Dad's advert flash up on the screen and quickly sped on. Once was enough.

I only planned to lay about for a little while and then do some revision, but before I knew it, I was engrossed in an old black-and-white movie. I watched it to the end, then went upstairs to shower. Then I planned to do some revision. But after my shower I was hungry again, so I went back downstairs and found some crisps and a chocolate chip cookie.

Dad came back from town carrying a carrier bag from an expensive clothes shop. You could tell it was expensive because the bag was made of thick shiny paper and had white cord in a loop for a handle.

"What do you think of this then, Cory?" he said, putting the bag on the kitchen table and pulling out a bright orange shirt decorated with little white stars. He held it against his chest. It was the kind of shirt that, if you looked at it for too long, might give you a migraine. I caught a glance at the price tag dangling from a button and gasped.

"What did you buy that for? You've got loads of shirts."

Dad turned and looked at his reflection in the kitchen window.

"I needed something for the *Daytime TV Awards* tomorrow. It's a big deal and I want to wear something that'll get me seen, you know?"

That shirt would certainly do that.

Dad turned back to face me. "What do you think? Looks good, yes?"

I wanted to tell him it was the worst shirt I had ever seen, but I just shrugged. I wished Mum was home but was glad she wasn't, all at the same time. Dad spending the money would have triggered another argument.

"I think I'll go and try it on with my suit," said Dad. He made for the door. "We'll grab some hot dogs for dinner at the fireworks tonight, shall we?"

"Sure."

He headed upstairs and not long after I followed him up and went to my room.

I played a few games on my phone and then listened to some music and a podcast about football and then I got a handful of treats and tried to teach Bingo to roll over. He attempted it a couple of times, but then settled his head on his paws and went to sleep. It wasn't long before Dad was shouting up the stairs that we'd be leaving for the fireworks in five minutes. I couldn't believe it! Why had I wasted so much time? But then I figured I still had tomorrow to get a load of revision done for the maths test. I'd just have to work extra hard.

It was getting dark when we left to walk to the top of Ivy Hill. Just like every year, crowds of people were heading in the same direction, but unlike when I was small, no one was interested in saying hello to Dad any more. Dad, however, seemed oblivious to this, and he smiled and waved at anyone who happened to look in his direction. Those that did look at him were more likely to be staring at the padded gold jacket that he was wearing rather than being interested in who he was. It was so cringy that I sped up to try and look like we weren't together.

"Whoa, slow down, Cory. It's going to be ages before the fireworks start."

"I just want us to get a good spot," I said.

I got to the top of the hill and I looked around for Rowan. I was keen to see him so that we could make a plan for the match tomorrow. I suspected he hadn't forgiven me for missing the game last week and that was why he was being weird and avoiding me. Although he had been like that for a while now.

Dad joined me, breathing heavily.

"Phew! That hill gets steeper every year, I'm sure!" he said, almost shouting. "Don't you think it's higher this year, Cory?"

A woman in a grey coat wearing a glow-in-the-dark necklace turned round to see who was being so loud. Dad grinned and waved at her, but she just stared, then whispered something to a man in a green padded jacket beside her. Why did Dad have to be so loud all the time?

"It's the same hill, Dad," I muttered, while keeping an eye out for Rowan. Still no sign.

"I'll go and get some hot dogs, shall I?" said Dad. He wandered off towards a van which had a giant hot dog on the roof and a long queue snaking away from its window.

It was becoming more crowded now and I spotted Agatha from my maths class standing with her family. Her mum was wearing a sparkly grey woollen beanie and she had her arm looped through Agatha's. There was a young girl sitting on her dad's shoulders who I guessed must be Agatha's little sister. She was eating a cookie and the crumbs showered down on to her dad's head making them all laugh. I felt a pang of envy in my chest. I wished my family were normal like them. Agatha spotted me and waved. I waved back then quickly looked away. I didn't want her to think I was staring. There was a gust of wind and I shivered, pulling the hood of my jumper up a little higher. Where was Rowan? A couple of kids ran past me waving some colourful flashing orbs that spun around. The lights danced around us. It was getting properly dark now, and when I looked up I could see hundreds of stars in the night sky. Dad came back with the hot dogs, a line of mustard and tomato sauce along each one.

"Here you are, Cory," said Dad. "By the way, the dress code is "formal" for the awards tomorrow, so I've ironed one of your shirts and hung it up in your wardrobe. I think that'll be fine with your school trousers."

"Right," I said, not really listening. I took a bite of my hot dog. This award ceremony was pointless, whatever it was. There was no way Dad was going to win anything. I licked some mustard from my fingers and took another bite.

"Thanks for coming with me, Cory. I know your mum has told you to come but, well, it means a lot." Dad sounded all serious for a change.

"S'all right," I mumbled.

"We'll need to be on the road by eleven thirty, so no lying in I'm afraid."

I coughed and almost choked on my hot dog.

"In the *morning*?" I said.

Dad grinned. "Of course in the morning. It's the *Daytime TV Awards*!"

I swallowed. It felt like a lump of bread was stuck halfway down my throat.

"But you said it was in the evening!"

Dad frowned. "No, I didn't."

"But I can't go in the morning. It's the cup final!"

Dad shrugged. "Sorry, Cory. There's nothing I can do about that. You said you'd be coming. Your mum has had to pull out because of work so I can't cancel another seat. There are some important people from the industry going! This is a big deal for me, son. I want some of my family there to support me."

"But I can't miss the match!" I yelled. "I missed it last week because of that pathetic supermarket thing."

A few heads turned to see what the shouting was about.

"Sorry, Cory, but you agreed to this weeks ago."

My mind was racing as I tried to remember. He was right. I *had* agreed.

"But I didn't know our team would get to the final then, did I?" I snapped.

Dad put his hand on my shoulder, a concerned look on his face which made me feel even more angry.

"Calm down, Cory," he said. "It's only a football match."

"But it's not just a football match, is it? If I don't go then Rowan will be angry and—"

"What will I be angry about?"

I turned around. Rowan was standing right behind me, a frown on his face. I opened my mouth but Dad butted in.

"Hello, Rowan. I'm so sorry but Cory can't go to the match with you tomorrow." He used his napkin to wipe a splodge of ketchup off his gold jacket.

"DAD!" I shouted.

"I'm sure you have someone else you can go with. That boy we met the other day at the supermarket, perhaps? I'm up for the Best Daytime TV Game Show Presenter award, you see. It's been in the diary for months."

He didn't wait for Rowan to answer.

"I'm just going to go and get another napkin," he said, scrunching the one he had into a ball.

Rowan folded his arms and stared at me. Over his shoulder I saw Will heading towards us. Could this get any worse?

"Is your dad being serious?" said Rowan. "Are you really cancelling on me? Again?"

"Ha!" said Will, overhearing. "Now *that* really is déjà vu!"

I ignored him.

"I'm so sorry, Rowan," I said. "This awards thing is really important for my dad and…"

"Mr 'Showbiz Smile' is up for an award? You are kidding me?" said Will. He grinned and pretended to hold up a trophy. "Thank you for voting for me as the Z-list celebrity of the year!"

"Shut up, Will," I said. But Will carried on.

"I'd like to thank my agent and the sunbed salon for giving me this orange glow."

"I said, shut up!"

"Oh and thank you to my dentist for whitening my teeth. Oops! It wasn't the toothpaste really!"

Will cracked up laughing. Seeing him take the

mickey out of my dad for the thousandth time made me see red. I edged towards him, not sure what I was going to do, exactly.

"Just shut up, Will!" I said.

Will looked at my face and took a step back and then, because we were on a slope, he lost his footing and fell on to his bum.

"HEY!" he yelled.

Rowan gasped. "Cory! What have you done?"

"I didn't do anything!" I said. "Are you all right?" I stepped towards Will, who was still lying on the ground, and reached out my hand to help him up. Will grabbed my hand and yanked me towards him.

"That's it, Cory Turner," he growled, quietly. "You have *had* it. On Monday I'm going to make sure no one talks to you ever, *ever* again."

He let go of my hand and sprang back to his feet. Rowan looked at me and shook his head, and then the two of them walked away, disappearing into the crowd.

I stood there, dazed by what had happened. How had everything gone so wrong within just a few seconds? I didn't know how he was going to make sure no one talked to me at school, but I did know Will Higgs had power. He would do it, all right, because everyone listened to him. School was bad enough. Now it was going to be completely and utterly unbearable.

Dad came back with a clean napkin, smiling as if he didn't have a care in the world.

"All right, Cory?" he said.

I turned my back on him.

There was a sudden *WHOOSH* and the crowd gasped as a rocket shot up into the sky signalling the beginning of the fireworks display.

I squeezed my eyes together, trying to hold back my tears. My stomach lurched when I thought of the week I'd soon be facing.

"I wish Monday would never come," I whispered to myself.

I opened my eyes and stared up at the rocket, now high in the sky – frozen for a second like a single bright star, before it exploded into a shower of shimmering purple sparks.

CHAPTER NINE

I woke up to the smell of burning toast.

I groaned. Dad was always fiddling with the setting on the toaster. I had told him so many times to leave the dial on four as that toasted the bread just perfectly, but he never listened and always ended up burning it, then finding it funny. Which it wasn't.

My alarm clock said 7.58 a.m. It was Sunday.

I put my arms over my eyes as everything that had happened last night came flooding back and hit me like a punch to the stomach.

Rowan clearly hated me.

Will was going to make sure no one spoke to me again.

And I only had one day before I had to go back to school. And that was going to be terrible. Plus I had a maths exam first period that I hadn't even begun to revise for.

But at least it wasn't Monday quite yet. I would definitely do some revision today. I just had to get Dad's annoying awards ceremony out of the way and then the rest of the day was mine.

There was a loud beeping sound – the burning toast had clearly set off our smoke alarm. I got out of bed and put on the clothes that I'd been wearing yesterday before heading downstairs. Dad was in the kitchen waving a tea towel at the beeping white box on the ceiling. I walked to the back door and opened it to let some of the smoke out.

"Morning, Cory!" Dad called cheerily above the loud beeping. "Can you take Bingo out for a walk? And when you get back, you'd better have a shower and get ready. Exciting, isn't it?"

I huffed. I took Bingo for a walk every Sunday morning, but I really wasn't in the mood today. I went to the hallway and stuffed my feet into my trainers. There was a shaft of sunlight coming through the window beside our front door. Bingo was asleep on the spot where the light hit the carpet. He always found the warmest spots.

"Come on, Bingo. Let's go," I said. Bingo didn't

move. His lips were fluttering as he slept, and I could see his eyes moving behind his eyelids where he was dreaming. His hearing wasn't that great any more and I clipped his lead on to his collar without him waking.

I patted his side. "Bingo, come on. Wake up. It's walkies time."

My old dog opened his eyes and pushed himself up, looking a bit dazed as to where he was and what was going on. When he saw it was me and that he was wearing his lead he began to wag his tail. I stroked his soft head and smiled at him. Bingo was very good at getting rid of bad moods without really doing anything. Just being a happy little dog was enough. He rested his head on my palm and I looked into his soft, milky eyes.

"You've got lots of weeing and sniffing to do. Your two favourite things! Shall we go?"

He shook himself awake and we headed out into the bright day.

I decided we'd go to the little park. That was Bingo's favourite place and I was pretty sure that to a dog, it probably had the best smells. My phone beeped. It was a message from Mum.

Hi darling! I hope you're having a lovely
weekend with your dad. Enjoy the awards
later and cheer him on for me! Everything is
fine here although it's really busy! M xxx

I quickly replied:

Yup.

I wished Mum was home so that she could go to the
awards. Then I could have gone to the match with
Rowan. Will wouldn't have said what he said about
Dad and fallen over and told me how miserable he
was going to make my life. My guts knotted again
with the stress of it all and I tried to push it out
of my mind.

The park was just a couple of streets away and the
entrance was flanked by two tall brick pillars and a
bright red dog-poo bin. On one of the pillars was a
sign declaring the rules of the park.

NO LITTERING.
NO CYCLING.
NO BARBECUES.
ALL DOGS ON LEADS.

Bingo and I walked towards the entrance when a bike skidded up behind us and a voice yelled: "Get out of the way!"

Glaring at me was a teenage boy on a bike. He was wearing a blue sports jacket, black gloves and a silver cycling helmet. He had a satchel slung over his shoulder.

"Move then!" he yelled. He tried to pedal around us but there wasn't enough room, and I had to press up against the brick pillar, edging Bingo to one side with my foot so that he didn't get squashed.

"There's no cycling allowed in the park!" I called after him. The boy sped on, weaving around a jogger who jumped out of his way. The jogger stopped, took out an earphone and yelled "Watch it!" after him, but the boy had already gone, disappearing behind the playground and into some woodland. The jogger shook her head, put her earphone back in and carried on jogging. There was a crisp wrapper on the path and her foot landed on it and she skidded and fell forwards on to her hands and knees.

"Ow," she said. I was going to help but she was quick to get back on her feet. Her knees were red from where she fell and she gave them a brush, then carried on her way.

Up ahead was the park cafe: a little white-bricked building with an outside hatch for ice creams and drinks and an inside area with seating. I could smell coffee and fried bacon. There were a few aluminium tables outside occupied by people eating breakfast and having a hot drink.

Bingo stopped for a particularly long sniff around a patch of yellowing grass and, as I waited, I stared at the customers. At one of the tables I spotted a couple I saw most Sunday mornings, who I called "the snoggers". They always walked around holding hands and staring at each other with silly grins on their faces. I saw them having a full-on snog on one of the benches once – hence the nickname. But from where I was standing, it looked like they were far from kissing. They were having a row.

"You've taken it the wrong way, Caroline," the man said loudly. "Why do you always jump to the wrong conclusion?"

"What was I supposed to think, Wayne? You don't tell me anything! You never talk. What am I? A mind-reader?"

In front of them were two tall glass mugs filled with steaming hot chocolate. I looked down at Bingo, pretending that I wasn't listening to their argument, even though it was pretty hard not to hear.

"Come on, Caroline. I haven't done anything wrong," said the man. "You have completely misunderstood me, yet again."

"Oh, just go home, Wayne," said the woman.

"Fine! I will!" said the man. He stood up and zipped his jacket right up to his neck. He paused for a moment, looking like he was going to say something else, but Caroline had her eyes fixed on her drink, which she began to stir with a long silver spoon. Wayne took a few steps away, then put his hand in his jacket pocket and took out a tiny black jewellery box, staring at it with a big frown on his face. It was the kind of box that usually held a ring inside.

"Ooh," I whispered to Bingo. "I bet he was going to propose!"

Wayne stuffed the box back into his pocket before storming off. When he'd gone, Caroline seemed to crumple a little. She put her hand to her face and wiped her eyes. Then she stood up and walked in the opposite direction to Wayne. The two hot chocolates were left untouched, steaming in the morning sun.

"Blimey, Bingo. It's all happening today," I said.

We carried on along the path a bit further and

then Bingo seemed to pick up a whiff of something in the air. He lifted his snout and delicately sniffed right then left. Then he pulled me towards the park pond where a woman, an older man and a little boy were feeding the ducks. There was a very low iron fence around the edge of the pond which was just the right height for Bingo to rest his head on. Bingo sat down, tail wagging as his nose twitched at the air. He didn't like water so there was no chance of him trying to scramble over the fence. I think he was hoping that a duck might come close enough for him to grab it in his jaws, but that was never going to happen.

The woman was wearing a long yellow raincoat and she had a paper bag full of duck food pellets which you could buy from the cafe. She threw a handful into the water.

"Look, Archie! Look at the ducks!" she said. The ducks went into a quacking frenzy, their wings beating the water.

The toddler was looking a bit bemused by the whole thing. He was wearing a knitted green hat that had pointed little wings on the side and a spiky tail that hung down at the back like a dragon's. I suddenly wished I was young enough to wear a dragon hat like that. When I was Archie's age my favourite thing to wear was a white T-shirt with a penguin on the front. One morning Mum couldn't get the T-shirt to go over my head. It reached as far as my ears but then she stopped.

"I think we'd better choose another top, Cory. You don't want to get stuck in it for ever, do you?" said Mum. I remember feeling so sad that I wouldn't be able to wear it again.

In Archie's left hand dangled a rather matted-looking, soft toy dragon. The ducks were really going wild for the pellets now and the older man pointed at them.

"It's ducks, Archie! Look!"

Adults can be so odd sometimes. They like to point out things even when you were right there seeing them for yourself.

The woman scattered another handful of food into the pond and then Archie suddenly held his stuffed dragon aloft and lobbed it towards the ducks, straight into the water.

The ducks flapped about a bit but were too interested in eating to be bothered about a toy dragon now floating around in the middle of them.

"Archie! Oh no! That's your favourite toy!" said the man.

"Oh, Archie! Granddad gave you that dragon," said the woman. "We'll never get it back now!"

Archie stared at the stuffed dragon which was rapidly soaking up water and slowly disappearing below the surface.

"Mine?" he said, reaching his arm towards the pond and looking at the woman.

"Yes, it was yours, Archie. But you threw it in! What did you do that for, darling?" said the older man.

The reality that he'd lost his dragon seemed to hit Archie and he began to cry, very loudly.

"MY DRAGON!" he screeched, running on the spot and reaching a hand towards the pond.

"Time to go, I think," I said to Bingo, who had dropped off to sleep with his head on the fence.

I scooped him up and he woke up and snuggled against me, happy to be carried.

We headed back to the entrance, but then I spotted something that made my stomach drop.

"Oh no. Not them," I said to myself. Will and Rowan were heading straight towards me. They were both wearing football scarves, but Will had his arm in a white sling tied around his neck. I thought about turning the other way, but I didn't have time to do a whole loop of the park. It would have been pointless anyway – Will had already seen me. They came to stop right in front of me.

"Well, if it isn't Mr *Déjà Vu* himself," said Will. "Waiting for us to see the damage you've caused, are you?"

I had no idea what he was talking about. I looked at Rowan but he was staring down at the pathway and scuffing his trainer against the tarmac. Bingo saw it was Rowan and began to wag his tail. He recognized him, even though he hadn't seen him in ages, but Rowan ignored him.

"What damage?" I asked.

Will rolled his eyes. "This!" He pointed at the sling around his neck. "You're lucky it ain't broken or my parents would be suing. My dad is livid! It's the county championships next weekend and I'm in three races. I'm not going to be able to swim now, am I?"

I was stunned into silence.

"My parents are going to call the school tomorrow and warn them about you. They need to know that they've got a 'problem' pupil in year seven."

"What?! Are you saying that *I* did that?" I pointed towards his arm and Will flinched and took a step back.

"Steady on there, cowboy," he said, shielding the bandaged arm. "I don't want you lashing out like you did last night."

"But I didn't touch you! You fell backwards and landed on your bum!"

Will shrugged.

"Rowan?" I pleaded. "You were there. I didn't do anything, did I?"

Rowan didn't look up. "I dunno. It was dark," he muttered.

Will's lips stretched into a smile. "I guess it'll be your word against mine at school tomorrow, won't it? And when everyone finds out what you've done, don't expect them to talk to you again, will you?"

I was gobsmacked. He'd said he'd make sure no one talked to me ever again and this was how he was going to do it! I looked at Rowan. We used to be best friends. Why was he letting Will make up lies like this? But Rowan was still staring at the ground. Will began to walk away.

"Come on, Rowan. We've got doughnuts to get before kick-off, remember?"

Rowan kept his head down and mumbled, "See ya later", and then they both walked off down the pathway.

I was devastated. Will was going to get me into the worst trouble at school and there was no way the teachers would believe me over him – especially if I'd supposedly ruined his chances in the swimming competition.

As if it wasn't bad enough already, Monday just looked a whole lot worse.

CHAPTER TEN

Dad drove us to the awards ceremony, and I slumped down as low as I possibly could in case anyone spotted me. The exhaust pipe did its usual embarrassing popping noise. I was still feeling anxious about my encounter with Will and Rowan. I was hurt that Rowan hadn't defended me, but I didn't want to fall out with him completely. He'd been my best friend for years and we usually got on really well and had a laugh. Ever since Will had come along it seemed our friendship had turned bad. And I *had* let him down by not going to the match. So, as we drove along, I sent him a text.

Really gutted I'm missing the match. Can you keep me updated with the score?

I saw that he'd read my message but he didn't reply. I waited for five minutes, then sent another.

> You don't believe I hurt Will's arm, do you?
> What was that about?!

Again I waited. Again there was no reply.

"Everything all right, Cory?" said Dad. "You're quiet this morning."

"I'm fine," I said. He nodded, satisfied with my answer.

Dad didn't seem to live in the same world as the rest of us. He lived on "planet showbiz" where it was supposedly acceptable to be paid in boxes of toothpaste. My issues at school would just confuse him. In his world everything was wonderful.

I thought about texting Mum, but there was nothing she could do about it from Spain. And besides, she'd already told me how busy she was.

"Well, this is exciting, isn't it?" said Dad as our car coughed and spluttered along the dual carriageway. "Do you know, I've got the old butterflies in the tummy. It's been a while since I've felt those! I think the last time was my first day on the soap. I do love acting, you know. Even more than TV presenting!

Although if I win the Best Daytime TV Game Show Presenter award then who knows where it might lead, eh?"

His laugh was almost as loud as the hideous orange shirt he was wearing that he'd bought yesterday. He'd teamed it with a black suit covered in tiny reflective discs that caught the light when he moved. I hadn't seen the suit before and guessed it was another expensive purchase that we could have done without.

"Do you win money?" I asked.

"What was that, Cory?" said Dad, glancing in the rearview mirror and checking his teeth.

"If you win the award today, do you get a cash prize?"

Dad laughed again. Why did he find everything funny? It was so annoying.

"No. There's no cash prize. It's the publicity that comes with winning that is the valuable part. If I win, I'll be able to get on the radar for some acting work."

I really couldn't see Dad winning. It was a miracle he'd been nominated in the first place.

I watched as all the other cars overtook us. We were going so slowly that one woman waved a fist at Dad as she drove past, but he just laughed and waved at her. Thankfully we didn't have to stay on the dual carriageway for long and we were soon on the edge of the city and then pulling into the theatre car park.

I got out of the car and waited while Dad checked his reflection in the mirror. The theatre was an old Victorian building with stone steps leading up to two wide doors which had long, shiny brass handles. On the steps I spotted someone famous.

"No way! Is that Johnnie Button over there?" I said, pointing. Dad peered over.

"Johnnie who?" he said.

"Johnnie Button! He's a radio DJ, model and influencer." I was quite impressed seeing someone like him here.

"Never heard of him," said Dad, taking off his seatbelt.

I watched as a young woman with a clipboard passed Johnnie Button a gold envelope. He was wearing a T-shirt splattered with rainbow splodges, a black blazer and light blue faded ripped jeans. He swept his hand through his long blonde fringe and then immediately dropped the envelope and stooped down to pick it up. A man with a face the colour of ham lolloped down the steps and the woman with the clipboard hurried after him.

Dad got out of the car and pointed to a woman standing by a silver sports car. "There's Sydney! Oh, I'm so pleased she came!"

Sydney Court was Dad's agent and the person who booked all his work. She looked very smart and was wearing wide-legged cream trousers and a short powder-blue jacket with dark sunglasses on top of her head. Beside her was a man who looked a bit like James Bond, dressed in a dark suit, white shirt and bow tie. I vaguely recognized him. The ham-coloured man walked over to Sydney, the woman with the clipboard hovering behind him. I guessed she must be his assistant.

Dad held his arm up and waved.

"Sydney! Yoo-hooo! I'm over here!" he called. A few heads turned to see who was being so loud. I cringed.

Sydney looked over at Dad. She whispered something to the ham-coloured man and he nodded and headed back to the steps leading up to the main doors of the theatre. Sydney pasted a big smile on her face and slowly walked towards us.

"Dennis!" she said. "You look fabulous." She turned her cheek and Dad gave her a kiss.

"It's lovely to see you, Sydney! It's been so long

since we've spoken," said Dad. "Thank you so much for coming to support me."

Sydney's eyebrows raised but she didn't say anything. I had the feeling she probably wasn't there for Dad.

"I've left you a few messages over the past few weeks about getting back into acting," said Dad. "Did you get them?"

Sydney looked up and tapped a manicured finger on her lip as she thought about it.

"I don't think so," she said. I could tell instantly that she was lying.

"Ah, well. Never mind," said Dad. "Anyway, isn't this great? It's such a shock getting nominated!"

"Hmmm. It's been a quiet year for game shows, I guess," muttered Sydney. She suddenly spotted me, standing beside Dad, and her angular eyebrows raised even higher on her forehead.

"My, my, haven't you grown, Rory?" she said, flatly.

"It's Cory," I said.

She ignored me and turned to Dad. "I need to go inside and find my seat."

"Of course! Us too," said Dad. We got to the doors where there was a small queue. Two members of theatre staff were checking off names and telling people where to sit. The guests all looked like they'd paid a lot of money for their outfits and I spotted a lot of dazzling jewellery and some impressive hairstyles but no one was wearing a bright orange shirt or a suit made of shiny discs.

"Sydney? Do you think I've got a chance of winning?" whispered Dad. "I haven't written a speech or anything, but if you think I'm in with a shot I'll—"

"I'd say you have exactly zero chance," interrupted Sydney. She was so rude! Yes, Dad was a little annoying sometimes, but he was one of her clients! Surely she shouldn't be talking to him like that?

"Sydney Court!" she barked at the woman who was ticking everyone off.

"Row A, seat 15," said the woman. Sydney strode off.

"Hello! It's Dennis and Cory Turner, please," said Dad.

The woman looked at her list. "Row V, seats 17 and 18," she said.

Dad thanked her and hurried on. We went through the large theatre doors into a dark foyer then through some more doors signposted "STALLS". There were rows and rows of padded red seats and the stage was awash with bright white lights.

Sydney was just ahead, stuck behind some people who were looking for their row. Dad tapped her on her shoulder and when she turned around I saw her roll her eyes.

"I know you didn't get the messages, but what I wanted to say was this is where I want to be. Back in the theatre!" He waved his hand around the auditorium, his eyes shining brightly. "I'm very grateful for the work that you've found for me so far. I mean, I like opening supermarkets but I thought—"

Sydney pressed the back of her hand to her forehead.

"Dennis. Now listen to me. You are not a theatre actor, darling. You never were. Your career is in Starlight toothpaste and opening Mega-Meals. You are what we in the trade call … mundane."

"Oh," said Dad.

"And that's not an insult," said Sydney. "It's a sign of reliability. You say yes to everything, Dennis. And that speaks volumes in this industry."

Dad looked puzzled for a moment and then he smiled. "At least I've got TV, eh? Now *that's* déjà vu!"

I cringed. Couldn't he see she was walking all over him?

A false smile spread across her face.

"Let's not discuss the future of your TV career, now, please, Dennis. There's a love. I really do need to go."

She turned and walked down the centre aisle towards the front row, then air-kissed the James Bond man before sitting down next to him.

We found row V and made our way to our seats.

"Why aren't you sitting at the front with Sydney?" I asked. "I bet the other nominees are up there too." It did seem a bit unfair.

Dad just shrugged. "Oh, it's perfectly fine here. We have a lovely view!"

By the side of the stage I spotted a photographer holding a camera with a long lens. She pointed it at a woman in the audience who immediately put her arm around the man beside her and they both posed. I had a worrying thought.

"This isn't going out on telly, is it, Dad?"

"Unfortunately not," said Dad, clearly disappointed. I, however, was very relieved to hear this. At least no one at school would see it and have something else to tease me about.

It wasn't long before the lights began to dim and the ham-coloured man who had been talking to Sydney in the car park walked out on to the stage and coughed into the microphone making everyone jump.

"Good afternoon, everyone. My name is Edward Wainwright and I am the director of the *Daytime TV Awards*."

There was a smattering of applause.

"Today we will be celebrating actors, presenters, news readers and many more people who grace our TV screens each daytime…"

I took my phone out of my pocket to see if Rowan had answered but I had zero messages. Dad prodded me with his elbow and I put my phone away.

"Let us start with Best Daytime TV Weather Reporter," said Edward. "And to read the nominees and announce the winner, please welcome to the stage TV vet and pet expert … Charlize Gander!"

The awards went on for ever. Those that won promised to keep their thank yous short, but they were lying and went on and on and on. The theatre seats were covered in a red, scratchy fabric which was really irritating and I was yearning to stand up and stretch my legs. Eventually, after what felt like a hundred hours, we got to the last award of the day.

"Now we move on to the Best Daytime TV Game Show Presenter," said Edward. Dad shuffled forwards in his seat and grinned, his white teeth bright in the dimmed lights.

"And here to read the nominations I am delighted to welcome to the stage radio DJ, model, actor and influencer – Johnnie Button!"

Johnnie, who was sat on the end of the row where Sydney was sitting, leapt out of his seat and skipped up the steps at the side of the stage.

"Hey, everyone! Nice to see you!" he shouted into the microphone.

Someone whooped and there was a bit of a buzz in the air now Johnnie had appeared.

"Right, so the three nominees for the Best Daytime TV Game Show Presenter award are … hang on a minute." He patted his blazer, and, for a moment, I thought he'd somehow managed to lose the envelope, but then he grinned and pulled it out of his pocket. The envelope glinted gold under the spotlights.

"I think I'll be needing this," he said. The audience laughed.

"The nominees for Best Daytime TV Game Show Presenter are: Tabitha Jackson from *Old Dog, New Tricks.*"

Everyone clapped and a few heads looked around, trying to spot Tabitha. A few rows from the front I saw a woman in a pale-yellow dress raise her hand to thank everyone.

Johnnie looked back at the card.

"Oh yeah! I remember this guy. So, the next nominee is Dennis Turner, presenter of the game show *Déjà Vu*."

The applause continued and everyone looked round again. Dad sat forward in his seat and waved his arm, just like Tabitha had, but because we were right at the back no one could see him.

"And finally, the presenter of *Your Cash, My Cash* … it's Timothy Gosling!"

That's who I recognized talking to Sydney in the car park! He was the man from the sports car advert that was on TV before Dad's toothpaste one. The applause continued and Timothy stood up and turned around, holding his arms up like he wanted to give the entire theatre a hug.

On stage, Johnnie opened the envelope and pulled out a small white card.

"And the winner is…" He took a dramatic pause. "Timothy Gosling!"

The theatre erupted as Timothy bounded up the steps and grabbed the golden trophy from Johnnie, shaking his hand vigorously. Sydney leapt out of her seat and clapped. I glanced at Dad to see if he was

OK with not winning. He was smiling and clapping.

"Thank you! Thank you so much. This was so unexpected," said Timothy from the stage. He waited for the applause to die down a little and then his face turned serious and moody looking.

"I want to thank my wonderful new agent, Sydney Court, for everything she has done for me and my career so far. You've been amazing."

Everyone clapped again and I saw Sydney blow him multiple kisses.

"*Your Cash, My Cash* has been a blast, but there are some even more exciting things to come, I can tell you!" said Timothy. "This is for each and every one of you!" He held the trophy aloft. "Thank you and goodbye!"

He walked down the steps and Sydney threw her arms around him. The awards director came back on and began to wrap things up, thanking everyone for coming. Dad leaned over to me.

"Right. Time for something to eat to celebrate, don't you think?" said Dad. "How about a pizza?"

I was confused. What were we celebrating, exactly? But I was never one to turn down a deep pan meat feast.

"Yeah, that sounds good," I said.

"Great!" said Dad, standing up. "Come on then.

Let's get going."

We crept along our row and out through the doors into the foyer. It was only when we were out in the daylight that I got to look at Dad properly. And I was pretty sure his grin wasn't as wide as usual.

CHAPTER ELEVEN

Dad drove us back towards home and parked outside the most popular restaurant in town – Pizza Palace. From your table you could watch the pizza dough being made and the chefs spinning it around their hands until it formed a perfect circle. They'd then smear the base with tomato sauce and put on the toppings before using a wooden paddle to shovel it into a wood-fired oven where the cheese bubbled next to the burning amber flames. The pizzas there were amazing.

We sat at a table in the middle of the restaurant and Dad took his phone out and texted Mum to let her know that he hadn't won. I spotted Agatha from school wearing a green T-shirt with "SAVE THE BEES" written on the front in yellow writing. She was sitting at a table near the window with her dad and her little sister was sitting on his lap and chewing on a pizza crust. Agatha was eating a really delicious looking strawberry sundae from a tall glass which had a pink paper umbrella sticking out of it. She saw me staring and nodded. I nodded back.

My stomach twisted. Seeing her again had reminded me that it was school tomorrow. And I still hadn't done any revision for the maths exam. I checked my phone to see if Rowan had replied to my texts from earlier. There was nothing. I tried again.

Hi Rowan. How was the match?

I could see that he was typing.

WE WON! 3–2!

I felt a mix of elation and total disappointment that I'd missed it.

Yay! That's amazing!

I waited to see if he was going to say anything else. He began to type.

The team are doing a victory parade through
the town next weekend.

I quickly replied.

That sounds great. Shall we go?

There was a long pause and then his answer appeared.

I'm going with Will. Soz.

Out of everyone at school, he had chosen to go with
the one person who hated me. Why? I didn't reply and
put my phone in my pocket.

Our pizzas arrived and I ate mine in silence.
Dad's phone rang and he jumped and quickly
answered it.

"Sydney!" he boomed. "It was so nice to see you
today. Thank you for coming!"

He paused for a moment and his face dropped a little.

"Oh yes, of course. Well, I'm sure Timothy was
grateful you were there for him, especially as he's a
new client and new to the game. Please tell him I said
congratulations!"

Dad's face looked serious and he was quiet and

nodded while Sydney spoke.

"That sounds like a lovely job. No, it's not last minute at all. Just email over the details and I'll be there. Will they pay for the train fare? Oh, right, I see."

Dad took a sip of his drink.

"And what is the fee for this one, Sydney?"

He nodded.

"Well, you know best, Sydney."

I groaned inwardly. What was he agreeing to do now?

Dad chuckled. "At least I'll have something to go along with the toothpaste, anyway!" he said, cheerily. "Oh, and Sydney, I know you aren't totally behind the idea, but could we have another chat about my return to the theatre? I really do think that—" He paused for a moment, then put his phone face down on the table.

"Oh. It looks like we got cut off," he said, quietly.

"Was she ringing with another booking?" I asked.

Dad sat up a little straighter. "Yes. And a very original one too! She said she forgot to tell me about it at the awards."

He took a big bite of pizza.

"Well?" I said. "What is it? What's the job?"

Dad frowned as he chewed. I waited and eventually he swallowed.

"I've been asked to open some new state-of-the-art public lavatories on the south coast. There's quite a stir about it by the locals, apparently, and the local TV news team are going to be there. So that's good!"

I couldn't believe it.

"You are being paid ... to open a *toilet*?" I said.

"Not a toilet, Cory. Lavatories." He wasn't smiling. I could tell that even he was struggling to see the positives in this one. If word got out that my dad had been booked to open a *toilet*, my life at school would be over. The taunts in the corridors would be horrendous. I could hear them already.

Hey, bog-boy!
I hear your dad's career is getting flushed
down the loo!
Is he going to be promoted to urinals
next year?

Dad continued. "They can't quite cover the train there. Budgets are so stretched these days! But the block is sponsored by a top brand of loo paper and—"

I put my head in my hands. I knew what was coming next. Dad was going to be paid in toilet paper. It was the toothpaste advert all over again! Dad must have seen my reaction and didn't bother to finish his sentence. We sat in silence until we'd eaten our food and our plates were empty.

"Would you like an ice cream?" said Dad.

I shook my head. "No," I said. "Can we just go home?"

As we drove home I thought about school and felt a tight ball of stress sitting high in my stomach just under my ribcage and resting on top of the undigested pizza. As soon as we got through the front door, I kicked off my trainers and went to find Bingo. He always made me feel better. He was like a superhero in dog form. I found him lying down by the sofa, his lips fluttering as he snored.

"Hello, Bingo," I whispered. "Can I stay home with you tomorrow?"

Bingo rolled on to his back and stretched his paws.

Dad was in the kitchen boiling the kettle for his evening chamomile tea.

I got up and called out, "I'm going to bed." I didn't wait for an answer and slowly thumped my way upstairs.

I went to my room and got everything ready for school. I packed my backpack then got my clean uniform from my wardrobe and draped it over the chair by my desk. I picked up my maths book and stared at the cover. I checked my watch. There was still time for some revision before bed. I sat down and flicked through some pages but then my phone buzzed in my pocket. Will had sent a message on the school group chat.

> Did you hear what Showbiz Smile Jr did to me at the fireworks? Cory is going to be in so much trouble tomorrow.

> No! What did he do?

> He practically broke my arm! My parents are going to talk to the head.

> What??

> You're kidding!

The messages flashed up, one after the other. All feeling sorry for Will and all of them being horrible about me. I tossed the maths book towards my backpack. There was no way I could do any revision now. And the messages kept coming. I turned my phone off and set my alarm clock for 7.30 a.m. Then I curled up into a ball and pulled my duvet up over my shoulder.

Monday morning was hurtling towards me.

And there was absolutely nothing I could do about it.

CHAPTER TWELVE

I woke up to the smell of burning toast.

I groaned. Again? Was Dad *really* going to nearly set the kitchen on fire two days running? I rolled over, keeping my eyes tightly shut. Maybe if I didn't open them then Monday wouldn't be here? And if there was no Monday then there'd be no school and no maths exam and no Will making my life miserable. A sudden, panicked thought ran through my brain and I opened my eyes, wide. My alarm hadn't gone off!

I peered over my duvet at my clock.

7.58 a.m.

School started in twenty-two minutes! Why hadn't Dad woken me up? Things were bad enough without me getting a late mark on the first day of the week.

I jumped out of bed and dived across my room to

grab my clothes. But the back of my chair was empty. My uniform was missing. I stood there for a moment and stared at the space where I'd left everything last night. Maybe Dad had popped into my room when I was asleep and thought it was dirty washing? I might be good at organizing myself the night before school, but I wasn't so great at putting my dirty clothes in the laundry bin.

The smoke alarm began to beep downstairs. Did Dad never learn?

Anyway, it didn't matter. I was late! I quickly found some more uniform in my wardrobe and got dressed. There was no time for a shower. I went to pick up my backpack but my hand found empty air. I looked around and saw it was upside down in the corner of my room. That was weird considering I'd packed it last night. Or maybe I'd dreamt I'd packed it? I didn't have time to worry about it so I stuffed in what I needed then ran to the bathroom and splashed water on my face before brushing my teeth in about ten seconds. I hurtled downstairs, jumping over Bingo who was laying in the morning sun in the hallway. When I got to the kitchen, Dad was waving a tea towel at the smoke alarm on the ceiling again. I frowned and shook my head, then I went to the back door and opened it.

"Morning Cory," called Dad above the loud beeping. "Can you take Bingo out for a walk? And when you get back, you'd better have a shower and get ready. Exciting, isn't it?"

What was he talking about? School wasn't exciting. And I never took Bingo out on a Monday morning. Dad carried on fanning the alarm.

"Why didn't you wake me, Dad? I'm going to be late!" Dad turned to me, a frown on his face. I huffed and went to the hallway. I got my school shoes out from the cupboard under the stairs and sat on the bottom step and began to untie the laces. Why were they always in a tight knot when I was in a rush? The smoke alarm stopped beeping and Dad came and stood by the front door, watching me.

"Cory? What are you doing?" he said.

"I'm going to school! And I'm late. My alarm didn't go off and you didn't wake me!"

I got my shoes on, picked up my backpack and threw it over my shoulder.

Dad had a funny smile on his face and then he erupted into laughter. I was getting angry. This was *not* funny. I was late and he was making me even later!

"Can you move out of the way so I can go?" I said.

Dad put his hand on my shoulder.

"But, Cory, it's Sunday," he said. "There is no school."

I stared at him, waiting for him to say something like, "Just kidding." But he didn't.

"Now, can you take Bingo out? And when you get home, you need to get ready for the awards ceremony. We haven't got that long before we need to leave."

He chuckled to himself as he headed back to the kitchen.

I stood there for a moment, wondering what on earth was going on. Was there an April Fool's Day in October?

I took my mobile out of my school blazer pocket and saw the time.

08:15 a.m.

My stomach really flipped then. School started in exactly five minutes, and it would take me at least ten to run there. I was the latest I had *ever* been! But then my eyes focused on the date, written above the time. My jaw dropped.

Sunday, 15th October

Not Monday. Sunday.

I looked at Bingo, lying happily in the sunshine. That was the same spot he was lying in yesterday morning.

"What is going on?" I said. I stared at the phone for a good few seconds, then rubbed my eyes and stared again. The date stayed the same. It was Sunday.

Dad put his head round the kitchen door.

"Come on, Cory. Chop, chop! Get out of your uniform and get that dog walked, please." He went back into the kitchen and I heard the kettle going on.

I swallowed. This was *so* weird. Was it really Sunday? Even though I was close to freaking out, I did notice that the tight ball of stress in my stomach had deflated ever so slightly. Did that mean there was no school?

I took my shoes off then went up to my room and looked at my phone again. There was another way I could check out what was going on. All I had to do was look for the messages that I'd sent to Rowan yesterday afternoon, asking him to let me know the score of the football match. And the one I'd sent asking him about Will's arm which he'd never answered.

I scrolled through.

They weren't there.

The message he'd eventually sent telling me

we'd won 3–2 wasn't there either. Or the one about the victory parade. I swiped the screen to find the messages from the school group chat: the horrible ones that Will sent last night about me hurting his arm which had made everyone pile in. Again, they were gone. It was as if everything from yesterday had been wiped from my phone in one big swoop.

I dropped my backpack on to the floor and slowly began to change out of my school uniform and into the clothes I'd worn yesterday. I felt like I was in a daze.

When I was ready, I went back downstairs and woke Bingo, clipping his lead on to his collar.

"Come on, Bingo," I said. "Let's go to the park, shall we? Again."

We headed down the road and then my phone beeped. I stopped and took it out of my pocket. It was a text from Mum.

Hi darling! I hope you're having a lovely weekend with your dad. Enjoy the awards later and cheer him on for me! Everything is fine here although it's really busy! M xxx

I stared at the message. It was identical to the one

she'd sent yesterday morning! This was seriously odd. What was going on? I put the phone into my pocket and we carried on towards the two tall brick pillars of the park entrance. Bingo stopped for a sniff. While I waited for him I thought about everything. Maybe Sunday hadn't happened at all? Maybe yesterday had just been a really long, very vivid dream? Didn't they call that lucid dreaming? Where you're asleep but you are aware that you're asleep. Or something like that. But that didn't sound right at all. Yesterday I hadn't felt like I was asleep and that everything was just a dream.

A bike skidded up behind us.

"Get out of the way!"

I spun around. Glaring at me was the same teenage boy. The one in a blue sports jacket, black gloves and silver cycling helmet. He shifted his satchel which was slung over his shoulder.

"Move then!" he yelled.

"I-I saw you yesterday!" I said, pointing at him. "You did *exactly* the same thing. You skidded and then you yelled at me then too!"

The boy grimaced. "You saw *nothing*. OK?" He put his foot on a pedal and I pulled Bingo out of the way and pressed my back against the brick pillar as he sped past.

And there was the jogger! He swerved around her.

"Watch it!" she shouted, her earphone in her hand. She shook her head, put her earphone back in and carried on, skidding on the crisp packet and falling on to her knees, exactly like before.

"This is so freaky, Bingo," I muttered. Bingo pulled me onwards and we headed towards the cafe, and then he stopped at a patch of yellowing grass. I must just be imagining it. I mean, I see the same people in the park all the time, right? So it was surely just one big coincidence that things seemed to be playing out exactly as they had done yesterday. I began to relax a little until I heard a voice.

"You've taken it the wrong way, Caroline. Why do you always jump to the wrong conclusion?"

It was Wayne and Caroline.

"What was I supposed to think, Wayne? You don't tell me anything! You never talk. What am I? A mind-reader?"

I looked over at the cafe. The snoggers were sitting at the same table with two tall glass mugs filled with hot chocolate.

"Come on, Caroline. I haven't done anything wrong," said the man. "You have completely misunderstood me, yet again."

"Oh, just go home, Wayne," said the woman.

My jaw must have been dangling open as a tiny fly flew into my mouth. I quickly spat it out. This was like watching a repeat of a TV show!

"Fine! I will!" said Wayne. Just like yesterday, he stood up and zipped his jacket right up to his neck. He took a few steps then put his hand inside his jacket pocket and took out the tiny black jewellery box he'd stared at yesterday. He stuffed the box back into his pocket before storming off towards the park entrance. Moments later, Caroline had dried her tears, stood up and left too.

This all felt much, much more than a coincidence. Maybe it was some kind of hoax? Was I being pranked? And if so, why? What was the point?

Bingo began to pull on his lead and I knew exactly where he was heading – the duck pond. When we got there I froze. It was exactly the same scene that I'd watched yesterday. There was a woman wearing a yellow raincoat throwing pellets into the pond and an older man holding a little boy's hand.

"Look, Archie! Look at the ducks!" said the woman in the raincoat. The ducks quacked and flapped around. Archie was wearing the same knitted hat, holding the same dragon toy in his left hand.

I stayed back, just watching them.

"It's ducks, Archie! Look!"

My heart was racing fast in my chest. This was so ... scary.

"I-I know what's going to happen next, Bingo," I whispered to my dog. "I know *exactly* what is going to happen."

As soon as I'd finished my sentence, little Archie raised his arm into the air and lobbed the dragon towards the ducks.

"Archie! Oh no! That's your favourite toy!" said the man. The woman and the man flapped around Archie, and the ducks flapped around the drowning dragon. I picked Bingo up and took a few steps backwards as the scene continued.

"Maybe ... maybe I'm a psychic or something?" I said, quietly. "Maybe I've somehow developed a way to see into the future."

Archie was at the crying stage now.

"MY DRAGON!" he screeched. His scrunched-up face turned pink and he had tears and snot running down his face as he stomped his little feet, his arm reaching towards the pond.

I was confused and scared and I wanted to go

home. I didn't like this one little bit.

Bingo rested his chin on my arm and I stroked the top of his head. When I looked up, Will and Rowan were heading towards me, Will with his arm in that ridiculous sling.

"Oh no. Not again," I groaned.

"Well, if it isn't Mr *Déjà Vu* himself," said Will. "Waiting for us to see the damage you've caused, are you?"

I looked at Rowan who was avoiding my gaze, just like before.

"I didn't hurt your arm, Will," I said. "I didn't go anywhere near you."

"You do realize you've ruined the county championships for me, don't you? It's next weekend! I can't swim like this."

He went on to say exactly what he'd said yesterday, about how lucky I was it wasn't broken and how much trouble I was going to be in when his parents rang the school tomorrow. Then he got to the part about how no one would want to talk to me ever again once they'd heard about what I'd done.

I was too upset to say anything. I just wanted to get home.

"I've gotta go," I said, hurrying past them.

"Oh, that's it. Run away!" said Will. "I am bringing you down, Cory Turner! DOWN!"

I held Bingo a little tighter as we walked. I spotted more things that I'd seen yesterday but hadn't really taken notice of – a boy learning to skateboard while holding on to his dad's hand, an older woman bending over to pick up her dog's poo in a green bag, a toddler sitting on her dad's shoulders.

I didn't want to see any more, so I kept my eyes focused on the ground until we came out of the park entrance.

I stopped for a moment and took a deep breath.

"I don't know what is going on," I said. "But I've a feeling we're not in Kansas any more, Bingo."

CHAPTER THIRTEEN

When I got home, I unclipped Bingo's lead and he automatically headed to his food bowl to see if anything had miraculously appeared in it while we'd been out. Dad was in the kitchen ironing his new shirt. His sequinned suit was on a hanger on one of the kitchen cabinet doors.

"You'd better jump in the shower, Cory. We've got to leave soon," Dad said, not looking up.

I hesitated by the door.

"Dad? Have you ever felt like you've done something before?" I asked.

Dad pressed the steam button on the iron and there was a big whooshing sound which made me jump.

"I've certainly used this iron a few times, I can tell you!" said Dad.

"I don't mean doing the same thing over again. I mean like you've lived the moment already."

He looked at me and his face stretched into his "TV grin".

"Now *that's* déjà vu!" he said. "Everyone gets that for a split second or so."

"Yes, I know about déjà vu, but what about … what about if you feel like you've already lived a whole day?"

Dad laughed and pressed the steam button on the iron again. "No. That's not something that happens," he said. He glanced at the clock on our oven. "Come on, get in the shower and changed please."

I traipsed upstairs and slowly got myself ready. When I went back down again I watched as Dad did all the same things that he'd done yesterday – checked that he'd locked the back door, took his car keys off of the hook on the wall, gave Bingo a goodbye pat on the head.

On the way to the awards I wondered whether to text Rowan, asking him to let me know the score. If things carried on as they were then I had a pretty good idea what the score was going to be, but I still wanted Rowan to know I cared. Today was just a blip and everything would be back to normal tomorrow, I was certain of it. I typed:

Sorry I'm missing the match. Have fun.

I put my phone into my pocket. I knew he wouldn't reply.

On the drive to the theatre the car's exhaust pipe did the loud *POPS* in exactly the same spots as it had yesterday, and the same people jumped and clutched at their hearts.

"Well, this is exciting, isn't it?" said Dad. "Do you know, I've got the old butterflies in the tummy. It's been a while since I've felt those!"

"Not since you started in the soap?" I interrupted, remembering what he'd said yesterday.

Dad frowned. "Well, actually, yes! That's exactly right. If I win the Best Daytime TV Game Show Presenter award it might open a few doors, back to the acting world. You never know."

"Um, Dad? I think it might be a good idea not to get your hopes up too much," I said. Dad tapped his hands on the steering wheel.

"What's that?" he said.

"I mean don't get too excited. Someone else might win."

Dad smiled. "We'll see."

We pulled into the theatre car park and Dad

checked his reflection in the rearview mirror. I spotted Johnnie Button on the steps by the main doors with the brass handles. The woman with the clipboard passed him the gold envelope – the envelope which I was certain was going to state that the winner was Timothy Gosling. Johnnie ran his hand through his hair and dropped the envelope – just as before. The man the colour of a piece of ham – Edward Wainwright – went down the steps and over to talk to Sydney. She was standing by the sports car, whispering to Timothy. There really was something suspicious about her.

We got out of the car.

"There's Sydney! Oh, I'm so pleased she came!"

Dad began to wave.

"Sydney! Yoo-hooo! I'm over here!" Sydney whispered something to Edward Wainwright and then I noticed her passing him a small brown envelope which he quickly stuffed into his jacket. She walked towards us.

"Don't say anything about acting, Dad," I said through gritted teeth. "She's not interested, OK?"

"What are you talking about, Cory?" he said, under his breath. He held out his arms as Sydney approached us.

"Dennis!" said Sydney. "You look fabulous." Dad kissed her cheek then went on about how nice it was for her come and support him. I tugged his sleeve. I didn't want to see him make a fool of himself again.

"Come on, Dad. We need to go inside."

He ignored me. "I left you a few messages over the past few weeks about me getting back into acting. Did you get them?"

"Dad!" I said, pulling his sleeve again. Sydney spotted me and her eyebrows reached for the sky again.

"My, my, haven't you grown, Rory?"

"It's Cory, actually," I said. "And growing tends to happen when you're a kid."

"Cory!" said Dad, sharply. "There's no need to talk like that."

Sydney, however, seemed to find my response amusing and her lips made a very slight upwards curve.

She turned to Dad. "I need to go inside and find my seat," she said, bluntly.

"Of course! Us too," said Dad. "Let's go in."

We were given our seat numbers and I slowed down behind Dad. I didn't want to hear this part where Dad asked for any possibility of theatre auditions and Sydney's blunt answer. I headed to row

V and sat in my seat and then the reality of having to sit through hours and hours of the awards ceremony for the second time hit me. This was quite painful.

Dad joined me and commented on what good seats we had, which we clearly didn't. The photographer took some pictures and then the lights dimmed and the director of the awards ceremony, Edward Wainwright, appeared on the stage and coughed into the microphone making everyone jump. I sighed, then rested my head on the back of the seat and stared at the lighting rig above us. His voice droned on and I closed my eyes and tried to work out why everything was a repeat of yesterday. Maybe I was experiencing some rare, psychiatric phenomena? Like when people suddenly wake up one day and can speak Dutch or play the piano. Perhaps all I needed to do was to ride out the day, get a good night's sleep and then things would go back to normal tomorrow. I mean, this wasn't so bad really, was it? At least I had a second chance to do some maths revision which I'd completely failed at yesterday. Or was it yesterday? Isn't yesterday now today? I rubbed my forehead. This really was very complicated. I listened as the awards were handed out at what felt like a snail's pace, but I must have dozed off because the next thing I knew I was jolted awake by Dad elbowing me in the ribs.

"It's my award next!" he whispered.

"Oh, right," I said, blinking and sitting upright in my seat.

Everything happened as before with Johnnie Button skipping on to the stage and peering at everyone from under his thick, floppy fringe. He announced Timothy Gosling as the winner and Timothy made the same speech. While everyone was still clapping, I turned to Dad.

"Can we go home now?" I said. This time I was going to do my maths revision as soon as we got in.

Dad looked puzzled. "Home? But I thought we could go and get some pizzas now to celebrate? It's not every day your dad gets nominated for an award, is it?"

He did that smile again. The one that looked like a smile but didn't seem quite genuine. I felt a bit sorry for him, losing for a second time. Even if he didn't realize it. And besides, it seemed a shame to miss out on having another pizza.

"Sure. Sounds good," I said.

*

The diners in Pizza Palace were the same as before,

sitting in the same places and eating the same food. I decided I was going to choose exactly what I'd had yesterday – or whatever that day was. Dad texted Mum to let her know he hadn't won and I looked around the restaurant.

By the window I spotted Agatha wearing her green "SAVE THE BEES" T-shirt and eating her strawberry sundae with the little pink umbrella planted on the top. Her little sister was back on her dad's lap, chewing on the pizza crust. We nodded at each other, just like before.

I checked my phone to see if Rowan had messaged. It was around now that I'd asked him about the match and I wasn't sure if I should do it again or not. I decided I would.

Hi Rowan. What was the score?

I could see him typing.

WE WON! 3–2!

Exactly as I had predicted.

That's great!

He was typing again and I knew exactly what he was going to say.

> The team are doing a victory parade through the town next weekend.

I was about to reply about us going together, but then I knew he'd already made plans to go with Will. So I just sent a thumbs up emoji.

The pizza came while Dad was texting Mum and then he jumped when his phone rang.

"That's Sydney," I said, before thinking about it.

Dad looked at the screen and his eyebrows raised up.

"It is!" He quickly answered it. "Sydney! It was so nice to see you today. Thank you for coming!"

I slowly ate my pizza while Dad had the same conversation with his agent about his new booking opening the toilets. The call ended and he looked at me, probably expecting me to ask what the call was about, but I didn't want to hear it for a second time.

At the end of the meal Dad asked if I fancied an ice cream and this time I said yes. I might as well make the most of it, considering I said no the last time. I chose a scoop of chocolate and a scoop of vanilla with raspberry sauce.

When we got in, I found Bingo in the lounge by the sofa and gave him a long cuddle. My phone buzzed in my pocket. I'd almost forgotten about this part of the day – the part where I got the horrible messages on the group chat.

Did you hear what Showbiz Smile Jr did to me at the fireworks? Cory is going to be in so much trouble tomorrow.

I watched as the texts fired through, one after the other. I ignored them and opened Mum's text from this morning that I hadn't replied to.

Hi Mum. I miss you. x

I headed to the kitchen and said goodnight to Dad then went upstairs. I brushed my teeth and put my pyjamas on then packed my backpack ready for school tomorrow – just like I had before. Then I laid my school uniform over my chair.

"You'd better be there in the morning," I muttered. Although the thought of Monday morning made the tight ball of stress in my stomach begin to expand again. Yes, today had been scary in parts, and I really wasn't sure what had made it happen, but at least I had avoided school for another twenty-four hours. Now Monday was coming and I was just going to have to face it.

CHAPTER FOURTEEN

I woke up to the smell of burning toast.

I bolted upright.

"No, no, no!" I said out loud. I looked around my room in the dim light.

My backpack was upside down in the corner.

The chair where I'd left my school uniform was empty.

I closed my eyes then ever-so-slightly opened them and peeked at my alarm clock.

7.58 a.m.

"What on earth—?"

My heart began to race and I put my hand on my chest, feeling it pound against my palm.

"Right. Calm down, Cory," I said to myself. "This

is just an incredible coincidence. This is Monday. It has got to be. And I'm late!"

I gasped as our smoke alarm began beeping furiously.

It was happening again. I grabbed my phone and turned it on.

The screen was black for a few seconds and then it lit up and there was the date.

Sunday, 15th October

My guts lurched and I clamped my hand to my mouth. I was going to be sick. I dived out of bed and ran to the bathroom. I got to the toilet and lifted up the seat and retched a couple of times, but nothing came up. I stayed on the cold bathroom floor, my head spinning. What was happening to me? Was I ill? Had something gone wrong in my brain? The smoke alarm kept beeping on and on and on and I put my hands over my ears to block it out. Why was it Sunday again? Why wasn't Monday coming? What was going on? Eventually the smoke alarm stopped and I took my hands away from my ears.

The house was silent.

I jumped when there was a knock on the bathroom door.

"Morning, Cory." It was Dad. "Can you take Bingo out for a walk? And when you get back, you'd better have a shower and get ready. Exciting, isn't it?"

I felt warm tears flood my eyes as I listened to Dad saying the same thing for the third time.

"Cory? Are you OK?" said Dad. He knocked again. "Can I come in?"

I didn't reply and the bathroom door slowly opened. When Dad saw me he immediately dropped beside me on to his knees and put a hand against my cheek.

"What's wrong? Are you sick?"

My tears began to fall then.

"I-I don't ... feel very well," I said through the sobs.

Dad moved his hand to my forehead. "You don't have a fever. But you do look very pale. Come on. Let's get you up and back to bed, shall we?"

He put an arm around me and we slowly made our way back to my room. He straightened out the bottom sheet and I climbed in under my duvet, then he sat on the end of the bed.

"Feeling a bit grim, are you?"

I nodded.

"What are your symptoms?" he said.

I thought about telling him exactly what was

wrong: that I'd lived through this Sunday twice now, and here it was again a third time. But I was frightened to say it out loud. Reliving the same day over and over must be a very serious condition, mustn't it? They'd probably need to take me into hospital and stick wires on my head or something.

"I've got a headache," I said. Which was true. "I feel dizzy and my stomach is in knots." Again, both true.

"Oh dear. That is really bad news. You know what this means, don't you?" said Dad. He looked so worried I thought I might throw up for real this time. I shook my head. "It means you'll have to miss the awards ceremony this afternoon. I'm so sorry."

I felt the faint flicker of a smile but quickly dropped the corners of my mouth in case it looked bad.

"I'm sorry, Dad," I said. "I know you really wanted me there."

"Oh well. It can't be helped," he said. "I'd better take Bingo out for a walk then get ready. Do you need anything?"

I thought about it.

"Can you bring Bingo up after his walk? He can keep me company," I said.

Dad smiled and patted me on the head. "Of

course," he said. "And I'll get you some snacks in case you feel hungry a bit later on."

That didn't sound so bad. "Thanks, Dad," I said.

He left my room and I lay back and stared up at my ceiling. I thought of the walk in the park that I was supposed to be taking right now with Bingo. There would be the speeding boy on the bike, the jogger falling over and Caroline and Wayne having their argument outside the cafe. Little Archie would be throwing his toy dragon into the pond and then Will and Rowan would turn up to give me grief. The awards ceremony was going to be happening this afternoon and go on and on and on, but this time I was going to be chilling at home. So even though the day was on repeat, it was clear that I didn't have to do everything that I had done on the original one.

My phone beeped. It was the text from Mum wishing me a nice weekend and saying how busy she was. This time I replied:

Hi, Mum. I hope it's OK there. I'm in bed as I don't feel too good. x

Big mistake.

As soon as I hit send I got a flood of messages from

Mum asking me what was wrong and what symptoms did I have and had Dad taken my temperature? She then threatened to actually call me, so I quickly wrote back that it was just a headache and I was fine.

A while later, Dad came in and deposited Bingo on to my carpet. He had his orange shirt draped over an arm.

"How are you feeling?" said Dad.

Staying at home was beginning to feel like the better option for the day so I shrugged as if it was too much effort to describe all my symptoms. Dad pressed his lips together and shook his head. "Perhaps I shouldn't go. I should stay here with you and make sure you're OK."

"No! You can't miss the awards, Dad. I'll be fine, honestly. And besides, I've got Bingo to look after me."

Bingo put his two front paws up on to my bed and I reached down and helped him up. He scraped at the duvet and walked around in a circle a few times before curling into a little comma shape at the foot of my mattress.

Dad nodded and checked his watch. "All right. I'll go and get ready and see how you are in a bit." Dad left and I gave Bingo a tickle on his tummy.

"We'll be all right, won't we, Bingo?" I said, and he

let out a contented sigh.

It wasn't long before Dad reappeared with a tray piled high with drinks, some sandwiches and fruit. He put the tray on my desk.

"Here are a few bits if you get hungry. I'll come home straight after the awards ceremony, but call me if you feel any worse, won't you?"

"I will," I said. He stood by the doorway, staring at me. I suddenly felt sorry for him. He was going to lose the award and he wouldn't have me to go to Pizza Palace with afterwards.

"When you see Sydney in the car park don't bother talking to her," I blurted out.

"Sydney?" said Dad. "Why wouldn't I talk to her? Besides, I don't think she's coming. She's not answered my messages."

I wondered what he'd think when he saw her in the car park in approximately thirty-five minutes.

After a few more "Are you really sure you're OK?", Dad left and I heard the car *POP* as he reversed off the driveway. The house was quiet at last, apart from Bingo's gentle snoring. I was suddenly really hungry so I grabbed one of the sandwiches from the tray and propped myself up on my pillows. Bingo's nose twitched and he lifted his head in my direction, his eyes still closed, then he flopped his head back down again. I worried a lot about Bingo. He was getting really old now and, even though there was a record-breaking dog who had recently had his thirtieth birthday, I didn't think he was going to reach that kind of number. I felt a lump in my throat just thinking about it, and I reached down and patted him on his bottom.

"At least you're not getting any older today, hey, Bingo?" I said. "You've had two extra days already!"

I finished my sandwich and lay back on my pillows. There was a gap in my curtains, and I watched some molecules of dust dancing around in the sunlight. I guess it could be worse. I could be reliving a day with torrential rain or when I had the flu or something. I didn't have to face Will and Rowan in the park or sit through the awards. I had a whole day to do exactly what I wanted.

I decided that first I'd watch a film, then I'd do some gaming and then, after I'd ventured downstairs for some biscuits, I'd do a bit of maths revision. Days don't get stuck like this forever and it was most definitely going to be Monday tomorrow, but for now I would just make the best of it.

*

I spent the day lazing around until Dad came

home. He came straight up to my room to check on me. He was early so must have decided not to go for a pizza on his own.

"How was it?" I asked. Knowing exactly how it was.

Dad shrugged. "It was all right. Sydney came! But I didn't win. Anyway, how are you doing?"

He sat down on the end of my bed.

"I'm feeling better now," I said. Dad smiled and nodded, but he really did look quite low.

"I wished you'd won and not Timothy," I said.

"Oh, have you heard he's won then? I didn't say, did I?"

"No. I, er, saw it on social media."

Dad stood up and took my tray which was now empty of food and drinks.

"Are you hungry?" he asked. I nodded. "Shall I order in a pizza?"

I grinned. "That sounds great!"

I pulled on my dressing gown and went down to the lounge. While Dad was in the kitchen phoning through our order, I turned on the TV. A woman wearing a gold-coloured trouser suit was grinning at the camera.

"Remember! If you match all six balls on tonight's lottery draw, then you could win five million pounds!"

A clear plastic drum filled with multicoloured ping-pong balls with numbers on them began to whirl and the balls jumped and spun around.

One of the balls was picked out by a tube which lifted it to the top of the drum. The presenter reached through a small hole and picked it up.

"And the first number is … twenty-two!"

She placed it on a stand. The next ball came up and she did the same.

"And we have number thirty-six!"

Again she placed it on the stand. Dad came in.

"I guessed you wanted a meat feast so—"

"Ssshhhh!" I said, sharply. "I need to watch this!"

Dad frowned. "The lottery? But we don't do the lottery. And you're not old enough for a start."

I waved for him to be quiet until all the balls were placed on the stand.

"I'll go and get some drinks ready," muttered Dad. He left the room and I sat forward on the sofa.

"Your lucky six numbers for this week's lottery draw are … SEVEN, ELEVEN, EIGHTEEN, TWENTY, TWENTY-TWO and THIRTY-SIX!"

The camera zoomed in on the balls so all six numbers were showing. I grabbed my phone from my dressing gown pocket and quickly took a photo of the

TV screen. The presenter thanked us for joining and then the music started and the credits began to roll. I sat back on the sofa and stared at the photograph of the six winning lottery numbers on my phone. I was pretty certain that things were going to go back to normal when I woke up tomorrow. My alarm would go off at the usual time and I'd be heading to school, anxious about the maths exam and having to face Will and whatever trouble he had got me in to.

But if they didn't, if it was Sunday again, I had something most people could only ever dream of having: the six numbers for the lottery that was going to be drawn that evening to win five million pounds. I felt my face stretch into a wide grin as Dad came in with two glasses of lemonade and placed them on the coffee table.

"Everything all right, Cory?" he said.

I reached towards the table and took a sip of my drink. The bubbles fizzled in my mouth and tickled my nose.

"Yep," I said to Dad. "Everything is fine."

CHAPTER FIFTEEN

As soon as I woke I sniffed at the air. Was the smell the same? It was hard to tell, but I thought I could pick up a whiff of something. My face stretched into a smile.

It was.

It was the smell of burning toast.

I looked at my alarm clock.

7.58 a.m.

Then I checked my phone.

Sunday, 15th October

It was happening again! Monday morning hadn't arrived. But this time I didn't feel sick. Today was going to be different because I had the winning lottery numbers! Saved on my phone!

I swiped to my photos to look at the picture I'd taken of the TV screen last night. But the most recent photo was one I'd taken last week, of Bingo lying on his back with his gums stretched back like he was laughing.

The smoke alarm began to beep downstairs.

I frantically swiped back and forth.

"Where is it? It must be here somewhere!" I said. But the photo had simply vanished. It was as if it had never been taken in the first place.

I put my hand to my face.

"Of course," I said. "Everything just resets itself."

I dived out of bed and grabbed a piece of paper and a pencil. I had to write the numbers down before I forgot them.

"Right, so there was an eleven, a twenty, um … a thirty-six." I wrote each one down and tried to picture the brightly coloured balls in my head. "A seven and an eighteen."

I counted them. I had five. What was the other number? I shut my eyes and tried to visualize the TV screen. What was it?! If I didn't appear downstairs soon, Dad would be knocking on my door asking me to take Bingo for a walk. I could pretend to be sick again? Another day of lazing around was quite tempting. And there was an unopened packet of custard creams in the cupboard that I could tuck into. Or I could do this day a little differently.

When I thought about it, this *could* be seen as an incredible gift. There was no school, no maths exam, no Will Higgs making my life miserable, no "Now *that's* déjà vu!" being shouted at me in the corridors.

And I had a huge advantage. I knew exactly what was going to happen today – what everyone was going to say and do. The day was already mapped out and *I* held the compass. And to top it off I had the winning numbers to the lottery! Well, almost. I was certain that the missing number would come to me any moment now.

I pulled on some jeans and a T-shirt and ran downstairs. Dad was waving a tea towel at the smoke alarm. I opened the back door.

"Morning, Cory," said Dad. "Can you—"

I put my hand up to stop him.

"How about I take Bingo out?" I said loudly over the beeping. "I can get ready when I get home. Does that sound OK?"

Dad looked at me. "That's exactly what I was going to say. How odd."

I grabbed a banana and began to peel it.

"I was thinking that maybe we could go to Pizza Palace after the awards?" I said, taking a big bite of the banana. The smoke alarm stopped beeping.

Dad frowned at me then laughed. "Sure! I was just thinking the same thing."

"Great!" I said. "I'll see you later. I've got a few things to do while I'm out."

I pulled my trainers on and got Bingo clipped on to his lead, and we stepped out into the sunlight. This was going to be fun!

We got to the park entrance and I checked my watch and waited.

"He'll be here any second."

A bit further down the road, and pedalling furiously towards me, was the boy in the blue jacket and silver helmet. What *was* he trying to get away from?

As he got closer, I saw his mouth open, ready to shout at me to get out of his way, but before he did I stood in front of the park entrance and held up my hand, like a police officer directing traffic. He screeched to a halt.

"What are you doing?" he yelled. "Move!"

I pointed at the sign on the pillar.

"There is no cycling allowed in the park," I said.

"There are joggers and children and dogs around. You are going to cause an accident."

The boy stared at me, then glanced behind him, clearly checking for something or someone. What was he up to?

"Forget it," he said. He pushed his foot on a pedal and headed off around the side of the park.

"First mission complete. Come on, Bingo," I said.

I spotted the jogger wearing the white earphones and quickly jumped forwards and bent down to snatch up the crisp bag that was on the path in her way. She looked at me, a bit puzzled, then smiled as she worked out that stepping on the rubbish would have made her slip.

"Thanks!" she said, running off.

"You're welcome!" I called back at her.

"Right, now for mission three," I said. "This could be a tricky one."

As we got closer to the cafe, I let Bingo have a brief sniff of the yellow patch of grass before picking him up and cradling him under my arm. The couple sitting at the aluminium table had their mugs of steaming hot chocolate in front of them. They hadn't begun to argue but they both looked thoroughly miserable.

They looked up as I approached.

"Hi there!" I said. "It's Wayne, isn't it? And Caroline?"

Wayne looked at Caroline, then back at me.

"Yes," he said. "Do we know you?"

I shook my head. "No," I said. "But I have something I need to tell you and it's really important that you listen very carefully, OK?"

They looked at each other, confused.

"You're going to have an argument in a minute. I mean, I'm no relationship expert, but even I can sense the tension in the air. Am I right?"

Caroline and Wayne were clearly baffled.

"I want to tell you that whatever you're about to row about, it probably isn't worth it."

I turned to Wayne. "Wayne? You've been planning this moment for a while, haven't you?"

Wayne opened his mouth and closed it again, then slowly nodded.

"Hang on a minute. How do you know my name?" he said.

I ignored him.

"Caroline? You need to ask Wayne what he has in his pocket."

Caroline frowned at me, then looked at Wayne.

"What is he talking about, Wayne?" she said.

Wayne was wide-eyed and his cheeks flushed pink. He seemed to be stunned into silence.

"This is your favourite spot in the park, isn't it, Caroline? You and Wayne come here most Sundays, I believe."

Caroline nodded but looked slightly scared by how much I knew.

"Over to you, Wayne," I said. "This is your moment. Go on!"

"I … well, I wasn't planning on doing it like this … but…" Wayne reached into his jacket pocket and pulled out the small black box.

"Here goes," he said. Taking a deep breath, he got off his seat and went down on one knee.

"Wayne! What are you doing?" said Caroline, her voice high and excited.

I smiled and walked away. Within a few seconds I heard Caroline shout:

"YES! OF COURSE I'LL MARRY YOU!" Mission three was complete.

"Right. Now for number four." I hurried towards the duck pond, worried I was going to be too late. I put Bingo down. The woman in the yellow coat was flinging the pellets at the ducks and enthusiastically telling little Archie to look at them as they quacked around in their eating frenzy. I could see the back of Archie's head in his knitted hat with the wings and tail. Dangling from his hand was his toy dragon which he began to swing back and forth.

"Oh no," I said, beginning to run. "If I can just—"

Archie swung his arm backwards and then launched the soft dragon. I leapt forward and snatched it, just before it landed in the pond.

"Gotcha!" I said.

The old man holding on to Archie's hand looked gobsmacked.

"My goodness! Where did you come from?" he said.

"It was like you appeared out of nowhere!" said Archie's mum, still gripping a handful of pellets. "If you hadn't caught that it would have ended up in the pond. Archie would have been devastated. Thank you so much!"

"You're welcome. Just doing my duty," I said. I felt an urge to do some kind of salute but managed to stop myself.

The soft dragon felt damp in my hand and I suspected Archie had been sucking on it, like toddlers do. He was staring up at me as if I were a superhero and had just swooped down from the sky to save the day. I held the dragon towards him.

"There you go, kid," I said. "Keep hold of it next time, would you?"

I gave him a wink and he grinned at me and then jumped up and down, waving his toy dragon at me.

I looked at the ducks, quacking and flapping excitedly. It was then that it hit me. The final number of the lottery!

"Two little ducks!" I said out loud. I remembered it was one of Dad's favourite bingo calls. The family stared at me.

"It's twenty-two!" I said. "The final number is two little ducks – twenty-two!" I picked Bingo up and gave him a squeeze and a kiss on the top of his head. "Thank you, Bingo," I said.

"I've gotta fly. Bye!" I said, then I pelted back towards the path as quickly as I could manage with a heavy Jack Russell under one arm.

This was FUN. My heart was pounding, the blood was racing through my body and I felt … alive! But then I saw Will and Rowan heading towards me and my stomach dropped. I could talk to them, tell Will that he was a liar and his hurt arm had nothing to do with me. But then, why face them when I could do the next best thing? Hide. I ducked behind a large tree trunk and watched as the two of them walked along, probably chatting about the match and how many doughnuts they were going to buy. They passed by and when they were nearly out of sight I trotted back down to the pathway and carried on towards home.

CHAPTER SIXTEEN

When I got in I went to the kitchen where Dad was ironing his shirt.

"Dad? Can you put some numbers on the lottery tonight?" I said.

Dad squirted some water from the iron on to a crease on a sleeve. "The lottery? But we don't do the lottery."

"I know. But can we try this once?"

I went to the kitchen counter and found a piece of paper and I wrote the numbers down nice and clearly.

I held the piece of paper up.

"You can take it out of my pocket money. Please? I've got a good feeling about this."

Dad carried on ironing. "I don't know, Cory. I'm not into all that lottery business. Money doesn't buy happiness, you know?"

I felt a bit panicky now. What if he didn't do it? I hadn't bargained on not being able to buy a ticket!

"No, but it would be handy though, wouldn't it? If we win you could do something good with the money. You could..." I thought about what Dad would choose. "I know! You could donate some to the Boxwick Theatre! They're always looking for funds, aren't they?"

The Boxwick Theatre was a little venue in town that always seemed to be struggling. Paint was flaking off the walls and the "C" in the theatre's name had been missing for years. I'd seen a poster outside just the other week asking for donations to help towards essential renovation work.

The mention of a theatre made Dad stop ironing for a moment and he stared out, wistfully, towards the fridge.

"I could get some more acting lessons," he said, almost to himself. "Method acting. That's what I want to try."

"Dad? The lottery?" I said.

He snapped out of his daydream and continued to iron.

"All right, Cory. Just this once. Leave the numbers on the table and I'll do it online when I've finished this. Now you need to go and get ready, please. We've not got long."

I slapped the piece of paper down and gave a little jump and a quiet "Yes!" before running upstairs to get showered and changed.

The thought of sitting through the entire awards ceremony for a third time didn't exactly fill me with joy, but as we pulled into the car park, my stomach was fluttering with butterflies. In just a few hours we would be millionaires! Multi-millionaires in fact! Everything went the same way as it had before. Sydney being rude, Dad asking about acting – although this time he mentioned having more lessons which made Sydney laugh out loud and say, "Really, Dennis? You'd be wasting your money."

While the awards were droning on, I made a list in my mind of all the things we could buy when we had five million pounds in the bank. So far I'd come up with:

A new games console.

A brand-new car that didn't make a popping sound every few metres.

A new cosy dog bed for Bingo.

A new house. Maybe with a swimming pool? And a gym.

Trainers.

I was so engrossed in my thoughts that Dad had to nudge me to applaud when the awards were handed out. Eventually we got to his category and Timothy Gosling bounded up to accept his award and make his speech.

When it was all over I turned to Dad.

"Pizza?"

"Pizza," he said.

Walking into Pizza Palace was like walking into a photograph that I had seen countless times. A chef was twirling the pizza dough on his hand. I knew he'd do it three times before placing it down and pressing it lightly with his fingers. Agatha was there in her green "SAVE THE BEES" T-shirt and her little sister was on her dad's lap, chewing on the crust of pizza.

We sat at our table and Dad texted Mum. I checked the time on my phone. The lottery results would be announced soon. I have usually texted Rowan around now, but this evening I wouldn't bother.

I stared at my menu and then I had a thought. I

was going to really make the most of this meal. So far I'd just had the same pizza but what was stopping me from having a few … extras?

The waiter came over and asked what we'd like. Dad asked for exactly what he had ordered before and when it was my turn I pretended to scan the menu, even though I knew it by heart, and told the waiter my choice.

"I'll have cheesy garlic bread, dough balls with a spicy dip and some barbecue chicken wings, please." The waiter wrote it down.

"Then I'll have a large Meaty Mayhem with extra sweetcorn, olives and mushrooms, some mozzarella sticks on the side and a large Coke. No ice. Thank you."

The waiter nodded and collected our menus then wandered off. That had cheered me up a little. I looked up at Dad who was staring at me.

"Blimey, son. That's a bit of a big order you've got going on there," said Dad.

I shrugged. "I'm hungry," I said, brightly.

But Dad shook his head. "The bill is going to work out expensive now, you know. Did you think about that?"

"It'll be fine. We'll be rich in a minute," I mumbled.

"What was that?" said Dad.

"Nothing."

My knees kept jiggling up and down. Dad finished texting Mum and the waiter came back with our drinks.

"Dad? If you won a lot on the lottery. Millions, I mean. How would you find out?"

Dad put his phone down.

"I think you get an email." His face spread into a smile. "I remember winning ten pounds once! That was back when it first started and everyone was doing it."

I grinned as I slurped on my cola. He was going to have the biggest shock of his life in a minute.

My mountain of food slowly began to arrive and I dived in. I managed the garlic bread and the chicken wings, but the pizza arrived before I'd even touched the dough balls and I realized that there was no way I'd be able to eat it all. I sat back in my seat for a little rest. I checked the time on my phone for the fifth time.

"Can you look at your emails now?" I said. I knew that Sydney was going to call him any second and I wanted him to find out the news first.

"I'm eating, Cory. It can wait," he said.

"I'll check for you then!" I held my hand out for his phone and he pushed it across the table towards me. I clicked on his emails and saw, at the very top, an email with the subject line: SOME IMPORTANT NEWS ABOUT A LOTTERY WIN.

Even though I knew it was going to happen I still felt shocked, and my heart pounded. I clicked on the email. The message was a bit of a blur and I struggled to take it all in, but I got the gist.

"Um. Dad?"

"What is it, Cory?" Dad was working his way through his second slice.

"You've got an email. Saying you need to call a number regarding a big lottery win."

Dad dropped his pizza on to his plate and wiped his hands on his napkin.

"Don't mess around now. Give me the phone."

I passed it back and Dad read the message, then looked at me.

"What is going on?" he said.

I clapped my hands together. "Ring them, Dad! Ring them right now!"

Dad's eyes were wide as he hit the number.

"Hello? Yes. Hello. My name is Dennis and I've received an email from you saying to call."

He listened to the person on the other end of the phone.

"I see. Yes. I see. Are … are you sure? OK. Yes. I'm fine. Yes. OK. Thank you."

He put the phone down and then he stood up and held his hands up in the air.

"I'VE JUST WON FIVE MILLION POUNDS!" he shouted.

At first there was a stunned silence from the restaurant and then people began to cheer and clap. A few people got up and shook his hand, including Agatha's dad.

"Congratulations, Dennis!" he said.

Agatha was staring at me, but she didn't look happy at all. She was frowning and had her arms folded. I guess that was to be expected – people were going to be envious now that we were mega rich.

Dad shouted out that he'd pay for everyone's dinner which made everyone cheer again.

"I need to ring your mum!" said Dad. When he spoke to her he began crying tears of joy. I pictured Mum on the other end, crying along with him. I wished she was here. When he got off the phone he saw that he had a voicemail from Sydney.

"You don't want to hear that. Trust me," I said. I grabbed Dad's phone and quickly deleted the message. He wouldn't be needing the toilet gig now.

Dad settled all the bills and left a large tip for the staff. There was another ripple of applause as we left and Dad waved and thanked everyone.

On the drive home we chatted about what we might buy. Just like me, Dad had a list, and his included a new house with a sound studio, a car and a new wardrobe of made-to-measure suits. Oh, and some method-acting lessons.

We got home and Bingo was in the hallway, waiting for us. Dad let him out into the back garden for a wee and I put the kettle on for Dad's chamomile tea.

"How did you know what numbers to pick? I mean, was it random? Did you have a premonition or something?" said Dad, standing at the back door and looking out into our dark garden.

"Erm," I said. "I had a dream and it felt real, so I thought it was worth a shot."

He looked at me, then came over and gave me a big bear hug.

"Thank you, Cory. I think you've just changed our lives for the better."

I squeezed him back.

I went to my room and got my bag packed ready for school tomorrow. My phone pinged.

It was a text from Mum.

I'LL RING YOU IN THE MORNING!

I smiled and wrote back.

SPEAK TOMORROW!

I got into my pyjamas and set my alarm and my phone pinged again, one after the other. This time it was messages on the school group chat.

Did you hear about Cory? His dad has won the lottery!!!!

OH WHAT?!

How much?

FIVE MILLION POUNDS!

YOU ARE JOKING?!?!

Hang on. Isn't he on this chat? Cory, is it true?

I smiled as I thought of Rowan and Will reading the messages that were now flooding my screen, desperate to know if we were now very, very rich.

Hi everyone.

I paused. There was another flood of questions, begging me to tell them if it was true or not.

What can I say? Yes. You're right. We are now multi-millionaires.

My phone went berserk as the messages flooded in. I smiled as I held the button to turn it off. They could wait until morning.

CHAPTER SEVENTEEN

When I woke my nose began to twitch. What was that I could smell? Was it something cooking? I sniffed again, half asleep, and then I pushed myself up.

It was the smell of burning toast.

"No, no, no, no, no," I said. I fumbled for my phone and switched it on.

"We are millionaires. This is Monday and we are millionaires."

My phone lit up and my shoulders dropped.

Sunday, 15th October

Downstairs the smoke alarm began to beep. I dived out of bed and ran downstairs where Dad was waving a tea towel at the ceiling.

"Dad! Dad!" I shouted over the beeping.

"Oh, morning, Cory," said Dad.

"Can I check something on your phone?" I said. He shrugged and I grabbed the phone from the table, quickly hitting the email icon.

"Where is it? Come on, it must be here somewhere."

"What's going on, Cory?" said Dad.

"I'm looking for an email from the lottery people," I said. "We've won five million pounds."

Dad laughed.

"Sounds like someone had a good dream last night." He carried on waving the tea towel. "Can you take Bingo out for a walk? And when you get back, you'd better have a shower and get ready. Exciting, isn't it?"

I put Dad's phone down. "No, Dad, it's not exciting at all. You've said all this to me loads of times! The awards are pointless!"

Dad stopped waving the tea towel. "Pointless?" he said.

I was on a roll now. "Yes. You won't win and Sydney will be rude to you. The whole thing is a complete waste of time!"

Dad looked shocked. "There's no need for that. How do you know I won't win?" he said. "And Sydney isn't rude to me."

"She is, Dad! She doesn't answer your calls and there is something about her that I really don't trust."

Dad shook his head. "You're wrong. Sydney is a great agent. It's not her fault I haven't been offered the best jobs of late. That's just the way the business goes sometimes."

I wasn't convinced. Her attitude towards Dad that made me feel like she wasn't being entirely truthful with him.

"Come on now, time to take Bingo out, please. Just because you don't want to come today doesn't mean you need to be rude. OK?" said Dad.

I huffed and went upstairs to get changed.

The morning was spent in the usual way, boy on bike, jogger, couple rowing, Archie and the dragon, Will and Rowan. I whizzed through all of it, not really paying much attention or caring a great deal. The more I thought about it, the more I wondered if Sydney *was* actually up to something. She had been whispering to Timothy in the car park before the awards. And hadn't she handed something to Edward Wainwright? I didn't trust her one little bit and I wanted to find out what was going on. When I got home I told Dad that we needed to leave ten minutes earlier because I'd heard some people in the park saying the roads were gridlocked.

"You don't want to be late for the ceremony, do you?" I said. Dad really didn't, so he got ready in super speedy time and we were soon on our way.

"The roads look perfectly fine to me," said Dad. "Are you sure there are delays?"

"That's what someone said in the park," I said. "It was something about temporary traffic lights and the whole area being at a standstill."

Dad frowned, expecting us to hit a traffic jam at any moment. But there wasn't anything and when we got to the car park it was mostly empty. There were a few parked cars but no sign of Sydney or Timothy.

"Well I don't know where you got the idea the traffic would be bad," he said. "We are far too early now."

"Sorry about that. I'm just going to go and take a look at the ... erm ... theatre," I said.

"OK, I'll be out in a minute," said Dad, completely distracted with checking his reflection in the rearview mirror.

I got out of the car and hurried over to the other side of the car park. I was hoping to listen in on

Sydney and Timothy's conversation, the one they were having at the time we usually arrived, but I couldn't see them anywhere. I was about to give up when I spotted a familiar looking silver-grey sports car. It was like the one from Timothy's advert. Sydney and Timothy were sitting in the front – Sydney was in the driving seat, so I assumed it was her car. They had the windows down and were deep in conversation. I walked around the cars and crouched down behind a large jeep to listen in. Fortunately, Timothy had one of those booming actor voices.

"I've not written a speech or anything. I thought I'd just see what I'm feeling when I have the award in my hands and what kind of vibe I'm getting from the audience," he said.

"That sounds perfect," said Sydney. "And it's great timing for the announcement about the *Déjà Vu* reboot next week."

My ears pricked up at the mention of Dad's TV show. What did that have to do with Timothy?

"I can't wait," drawled Timothy. "Obviously, if it was staying on that dreadful channel then I clearly wouldn't have touched it with a bargepole. But prime-time Saturday night telly? A brand-new set? An eye-watering fee for me? Yes please!"

I couldn't believe it! Dad was being fired! And Timothy was getting *his* job!

"It's all worked out so well, darling. Who would have thought that there's a new fan base for cheesy game shows? The ratings have been soaring. Even with Dennis at the helm! Moving it to a prime-time slot on a better channel with a young, new presenter. Well, it's a no-brainer."

What? Dad's show is actually popular? This was incredible news!

"It's a shame you had to pull a few strings for me to win this thing," said Timothy. "I must say, I do feel a little … uncomfortable about taking the trophy. Dennis did get the highest vote, after all."

"Oh, don't worry about that," snapped Sydney. "Dennis is a fading star. Yes, some of the old dears still like him and you know how old people like to vote in these kinds of things. But you, my dear, are a rising star. And this award is what we need to get that spotlight on you for a while. Before long everyone will have forgotten the name Dennis Turner."

Dad was the true winner?!

More cars were pulling into the car park now. I heard the windows of the sports car being closed and then the two of them got out. I stood a few metres behind them, pretending I was looking at something on my phone.

I spotted Johnnie Button on the steps of the theatre. He was running his hand through his blonde fringe and about to drop the envelope in one … two … three…

And there it was, on the floor. He bent down to pick it up.

Dad was just getting out of his car and Timothy and Sydney looked over at him.

"Does Dennis know he's lost the gig yet?" said Timothy.

"Not yet. I expect he'll dump me when he finds out, but I've got a few little gigs I want him to do first before I send him on his way. There aren't many clients who are foolish enough to accept toothpaste or loo rolls as a fee."

She leaned towards Timothy. "While I take the actual cash, of course!"

Timothy laughed then headed to the theatre entrance.

I gasped. Dad *was* being paid for those jobs but rather than his agent taking a small amount, she was pocketing the whole lot and just giving Dad the freebies that came with it! And if she was doing that then I suspected the money he got for *Déjà Vu* wasn't the proper amount either. She was a con artist!

The ham-coloured man – Edward Wainwright – walked over to Sydney, his assistant following close behind.

"Eddie!" said Sydney. "Are we all sorted?"

Edward nodded and mumbled something I couldn't make out. Then Sydney took an envelope out of her bag and passed it to Edward who looked a bit flustered and quickly stuffed it into the inside of his jacket. From this angle I could tell the envelope was filled with something. Was it cash? Dad called out from across the car park.

"Sydney! Yoo-hooo! I'm over here!"

Sydney looked across at Dad, then leaned closer to Edward.

"Thank you, Eddie. I knew I could trust you." She then pasted a big smile on her face and slowly walked towards Dad.

"Dennis!" she said. "You look fabulous."

I stood to one side while Dad talked to Sydney. She was horrible and manipulative, and Dad clearly had *no* idea. I had to warn him about her!

I followed them inside but went straight to my seat while Dad followed Sydney and tried to talk to her about his acting career. As soon as he shuffled along row V I launched into everything I'd just discovered.

"Dad! Sydney is ripping you off! You know the toothpaste advert? You were supposed to get a load of money for doing that, but she took it! She took the whole lot and you just ended up with toothpaste!"

Dad chuckled. "What are you talking about, Cory? Don't be silly."

"And that's not everything. Later on today she's going to ask you to open a new block of toilets. And you're going to be paid in loo rolls! She's conning you, Dad. You've got to sack her and find a new agent!"

Dad smiled at me as if I was a five-year-old.

"Cory, I've been with Sydney for over twenty years. She wouldn't do anything like that." He looked across the auditorium to the stage. The awards were about to start.

"I'm guessing that she's not giving you the full amount for presenting *Déjà Vu*, either! Did you know that it's actually really popular? The ratings are soaring!" I said, almost gasping as I tried to get it all out. "And, actually I'm really sorry about this bit but, Dad, you're going to be sacked! Timothy Gosling is going to be the new presenter on a new channel and for a lot of money."

"What? Why on earth would you say that?"

"Because it's true! He's here and I heard them talking!"

The lights began to dim and there was a ripple of applause.

"He's going to win the award tonight, Dad. But it's supposed to be you! You got the most votes, but Sydney has managed to fix the whole thing so he wins," I said through gritted teeth. "You've got to listen to me, Dad!"

Dad shot me a thunderous look.

"I don't know what you're trying to do here by making up these kinds of stories, Cory. Are you trying to get me to leave so you can go to that football match? Is that it?"

I opened my mouth wide. "No! It's got nothing to do with that!" I said. "Honestly, Dad. I'm telling the—"

The sound of coughing into a microphone made me jump.

"Good afternoon, everyone. My name is Edward Wainwright and I am the director of the *Daytime TV Awards*."

Dad faced forward, a smile back on his face as he watched the opening announcement for the awards. Why wouldn't he listen to me?

I sat back and folded my arms. How was I going to convince Dad that I was telling him the truth – that his agent was stealing from him. From us!

The awards went on and on and when it came to Dad's nomination, I watched his face as they announced the winner. I had told him that it was going to be Timothy, but he didn't react in the slightest. The ceremony ended and the audience gradually stood up and began to put on their coats and jackets. We stayed in our seats. Dad didn't say a word.

"So, what do you think, Dad? About what I said? Are you going to talk to Sydney?"

Dad blinked a few times then rubbed at his chin.

"I think that you need to take some time to think about what you've said to me this afternoon. I know you really wanted to go to that football match, but it was important for me to have you here. Making up stories like that, just to make me leave was—"

"But I didn't make it up! I heard them talking! She's been lying to you!"

Dad stood up and shook his head. "Come on, we're going."

We made our way back to the car and Dad began to drive. I thought that at least I had some pizza to look forward to, but when we got to the roundabout where Pizza Palace was, Dad turned left towards home.

"Aren't we going for pizza? To celebrate?" I said.

Dad screwed his eyebrows together. "Celebrate what exactly, Cory?"

He was so upbeat all the time that I didn't think I had ever heard Dad sound like this. He sounded defeated – like he'd had enough.

I'd had enough too. I didn't want to repeat this day ever again. I wanted things to go back to how they were – even if that meant going back to school, and maths tests and having to face Will. I also really, really missed my mum. If Monday never arrived, when would I see her again?

When we got in, Dad took the phone call from Sydney telling him about opening the toilet block – just as I had told him. He was as friendly and chatty as always. He did frown at me afterwards though, and pointed out that I'd clearly been snooping on other people's conversations and that wasn't on at all.

That night, when I went to bed, I decided I wouldn't pack my school bag or get my uniform ready. Maybe if I didn't do those things then that might help to put things right? And if Monday did arrive then I'd just have to get my stuff ready in the morning.

I got into bed and took my phone, not reading the barrage of messages on the group chat about how I'd supposedly hurt Will's arm.

I decided to send Mum a message.

I miss you, Mum. Hurry home. Please? x

I set my alarm clock, turned off my lamp and tried to go to sleep.

CHAPTER EIGHTEEN

I woke to the smell of burning toast and pushed myself up to sitting.

It was still Sunday.

I put my head in my hands and took some long deep breaths. I was stuck here. Again.

I leaned back on to my headboard and turned my phone on, hoping that I might have a reply from Mum to the message I'd sent her last night. But my message had vanished. I dropped my phone on to my lap and rubbed at my face. The smoke alarm began to beep. Very soon, Dad would be shouting up the stairs.

What was I going to do? This was starting to feel terrifying. I couldn't keep reliving the same day over and over for all of eternity! What about Mum? How was I going to see her again?

"Cory? Can you take Bingo out?" Dad yelled. "And when you get back, you'd better have a shower and get ready! Exciting, isn't it?"

I wasn't sure what to do. Maybe I could just run away? Maybe that would stop whatever was happening. Maybe I needed to get as far away from Boxwick as I could. Like to the other side of the world or something?

I got out of bed, pulled on my dressing gown and prepared myself to do my "I feel sick" routine for Dad. I felt guilty lying to him again but there was no other alternative.

I met Dad on the landing.

"Oh. You're not dressed," said Dad.

"I don't feel so good, Dad," I said. "I think I need to stay here today. I don't think I can come to the awards."

But this time Dad looked uncertain.

"Really, Cory? And this sudden illness doesn't have anything to do with a certain football match you're missing today, does it?"

I'd made an error by mentioning the awards straight away. Of course he thought it looked

172

suspicious! But in all honesty my stomach was churning again. And I felt a bit tearful. I wiped at my eyes.

"It's nothing to do with the football," I said quietly. "Honestly."

Dad looked at me closely.

"You do look a little peaky. Hmm. OK. Let's get you back into bed, shall we?"

I shuffled back to my room and Dad got ready to take Bingo for a walk and I heard the door close behind him.

Mum sent her usual text and this time I replied properly.

Hi Mum. I miss you. x

She sent a heart emoji back.

I had to come up with a plan but what could I do? I opened the search engine on my phone.

What to do if you're stuck in the same day?

But it just brought up information about changing your job or dumping a boyfriend. None of it was helpful. Every morning I woke up in my bed so I wondered if I went somewhere else, would that break the pattern? It sounded like a possibility. I could get as far away from here as possible to try and get back to Monday. But where should I go? Maybe I could get a flight to Madrid and find Mum? No. That wouldn't work. I was pretty sure you had to be over eighteen to buy a plane ticket. And anyway, I had no idea where my passport was or how I would even find Mum. Maybe a train somewhere far away would be best? I had some money saved up in my bank account so I could pay for a single ticket somewhere. I checked online for the trains from our local station and worked out I could probably get to Scotland with a couple of changes. Surely that would be enough to break the spell or whatever it was that kept making the day repeat?

I was a bit nervous about travelling so far. The furthest I'd been on my own was into town on the bus and back. Going all the way to another country felt scary. Should I pack a case? I wasn't sure. I couldn't do anything until Dad left for the awards so I just lay there, worrying about what I should do and what things I should take.

Dad came back from the dog walk and checked in on me.

"How are you doing, Cory?" said Dad. "Still feeling rough?"

I nodded and he sighed. He seemed reluctant to leave me, but once I'd reassured him that I'd be OK he went off to get changed. Before he left he came back in with a tray of food.

"Call or text if you need me. OK?" said Dad.

I nodded. He was just about to go when I called him back.

"Dad?"

He popped his head round the door.

"I hope it goes well. The awards, I mean," I said. "And it doesn't matter if you don't win."

Dad looked a bit puzzled. "Um. OK. Thanks for that, Cory. I'll see you later."

As soon as the front door closed and I heard the car reversing off the driveway, I dived out of bed and got dressed. I grabbed some cash from my money box and my bank card, my phone and my keys. I found a small sports bag and packed a charger and some of the food that Dad had left on the tray, then I went downstairs.

Bingo was curled up in his basket down by the washing machine in the kitchen and I gave him a quick tummy rub.

"Do you want to come too, Bingo?" I said. "It won't be as scary if you're with me."

But then I thought if Bingo came I'd have to pack some dog food and water. And maybe his favourite blanket. He really didn't like walking too far now, and I wasn't sure if I could carry all of my stuff and him as well.

"I think you'll have to stay here, Bingo. I've just got to go on a little trip and then we can get back to normal, eh?" He yawned and thumped his tail in appreciation.

The train station was too far to walk so I ran to the bus stop. There was a bus already there and I sprinted and got on just before the driver closed the door.

"In a rush, are we?" she said.

"Yep," I said, paying for my ticket. I sat downstairs, rested my head against the window and watched the people on the streets carrying on with their days. This was a Sunday that I hadn't seen before, repeating itself over and over while I relived my one. We passed the old theatre, and I noticed a plank of wood was blocking up one of the doors where the glass must have smashed. Alongside a poster asking for donations towards repairs, there was a big sign that read:

OPEN AUDITIONS!

**COULD YOU BE A CAST MEMBER FOR
OUR NEW PRODUCTION OF
AN INSPECTOR CALLS?**

We carried on and the bus pulled up at a stop outside the town library. I spotted Agatha coming down the library slope carrying an armful of books. She looked up and then stopped abruptly when she saw me staring at her through the window. The doors of the bus whooshed closed and we began to pull away, but Agatha was still staring. I thought that was a bit weird, but then something else caught my eye. It was the teenage boy on the bike from the park! The one that almost runs into me at the entrance. But now he was sitting on a bench with his bike propped up beside him. The satchel that had been slung across his shoulder was on his lap and he was looking inside at the contents. What was he up to?

The bus took for ever to get to the station as there were so many passengers getting on and off, but eventually we pulled up right outside.

"All change please. This is the last stop. All change."

The station was bustling with people. A girl

177

wearing a navy-blue baseball cap and carrying a backpack nearly as big as her came out of the entrance and a woman squealed and ran to give her a hug. I guessed she'd just got back from travelling somewhere far away. There was a sign for the ticket office but I didn't really want to talk to an adult in case they asked me lots of questions about why I was travelling so far on my own, so I wandered over to the ticket machine. It was really complicated with hundreds of buttons, but after a few tries I worked out how to buy a ticket for Edinburgh in Scotland. The price flashed up on the screen.

"How much?!" I said, loudly. I had no idea train tickets were so expensive! A woman wearing a train company uniform wandered over from the ticket barrier.

"Are you OK there, sir?" I'd never been called sir before. I quickly tapped my card on the payment square.

"Yes. I'm fine, thank you."

I saw from her name badge that she was called Brenda. She glanced at the screen on the ticket machine and frowned.

"You're going rather a long way," she said. "Do you have an adult accompanying you?"

I swallowed. I wasn't going to be stopped this early on, was I?

"Yes. My mum is getting on at the next station," I said.

The machine gave me my ticket and receipt and I fumbled with them to try and work out which one I needed to get through the barrier. Brenda was still watching me.

"Excuse me? Can you help? My ticket's not working." A passenger was trying to get through the barrier. Brenda gave me one more thoughtful look, then she went over to help the man.

While she was distracted, I quickly put my ticket in the slot and made my way to the platform. The train was due in two minutes and I kept checking around to see if Brenda was going to be there, wanting to ask me more questions. But she didn't appear. On one of the station walls was a film poster for a new comedy film. Dad's old acting friend, Martin, was one of the actors in it and his name was in bold letters right at the top. I kind of got why Mum was annoyed that Dad hadn't been as successful. It wasn't that she was greedy – she just felt that Dad was a brilliant actor too and deserved to have his chance.

When the train arrived, I got on and found a seat

in a corner by the luggage rack. There was a family sitting at a table not far from me, playing a game of cards. We pulled away and I watched the world pass from the window. I tried to relax and not think too much about what I would do when I got to Scotland. I had nowhere to stay for a start. Maybe I should have tried to book a hotel or something. But how would I pay? The train fare had used up my savings. And I had no way of paying for a return ticket, either. I just had to hope that this worked and I'd wake up in my bed tomorrow and it would be Monday morning.

I was distracted from worrying for a moment by the family sat at the table. They were playing a card game that I recognized as one that me, Mum and Dad used to play.

"Daddy! It's your go!" said the little girl.

"Right. Three aces," said the dad, putting some cards face down on the table.

"Cheat!" shouted the little girl.

The dad laughed and turned over his cards which were a two and an eight. "Ah! How do you always manage to see through me?" He picked up the big pile of cards that were in the middle of the table.

"Two sevens," said the mum.

"Two kings," said the girl.

"Cheat!" said the dad. The girl revealed her cards – two kings – and the dad groaned. He really wasn't very good at the game at all.

They carried on playing and were having so much fun that I was quite engrossed watching them. The mum caught me looking and smiled and I smiled back, then I turned away, resting my head on the window again. We hadn't played any games in our house for ages. In fact, we never really did anything together any more, unless you counted going along to support Dad for one of his "gigs". He never used to ask us to go when he was popular on TV and earning good money. Maybe he needed us to be there because he was … nervous in some way? He never looked nervous, but maybe he was good at hiding it or putting on an act. I saw a cartoon once about a clown who was fun and happy all the time, but behind closed doors he was sad and cried a lot. Maybe Dad was a bit like that too?

I watched as the scenery outside the window changed from large warehouses and blocks of flats to green fields and trees. I spotted some cows, swishing their tails as they ate the grass and then I saw a woman walking a chocolate-coloured Labrador who was wagging its tail happily. For a second I wished

I had brought Bingo after all. He'd have made me feel better.

My phone beeped. It was a message from Dad.

How are you doing, Cory? I thought I'd get
a pizza to bring home after the awards if
you're feeling up to it?

I stared at the words. When Dad got home I wouldn't be there and he would panic and think I'd gone missing or run away! He'd be frantic and would call the police. And then there would be a whole search party out looking for me! I hadn't thought this through. The consequences of what I was doing would be terrible. This was a huge mistake! I had to get back.

A guard was coming along the aisle.

"Tickets please. Any tickets."

When he got to me I showed him my ticket.

"How long is it until we get to the next stop?" I asked.

The guard checked his watch. "Twenty minutes."

"And can I get a train back to Boxwick from there?"

The guard frowned. "You can. But not with that ticket you've got there."

"Can I buy a ticket from you?" I asked, trying not

to let the panic show in my voice.

Behind him I could see the mum looking over.

"Certainly. I can do that for you now," said the guard. He pushed some buttons on the machine he was carrying on a strap around his neck. I tapped my bank card on the machine when he told me to, but he shook his head.

"Sorry. It's been declined. Try again."

I had another go, but it still didn't work. I didn't have enough money left in my account. Suddenly I felt like I might cry. What was I going to do? Just then, the mum who had been playing cards was standing behind the guard.

"Excuse me, can I help at all? Are you OK?"

She looked at me and I could see concern on her face.

"I need to go home and I don't have enough money." My eyes were warm with tears.

The guard was staring at his machine, frowning.

"Let me," said the mum. Before I could object she whipped out her bank card and tapped.

"Yup. That's gone through," said the guard, printing off the ticket and a receipt.

"Thank you," I said. But the mum just nodded and slipped back into her seat. It was so kind of her.

I could imagine Mum and Dad doing exactly the same thing for someone else and I vowed that when I was an adult, I'd do the same if I ever saw anyone needing help. I got home without any issues and was back in my room before Dad even got home so he was none the wiser. I was gutted that I'd failed, but I decided that travelling across the country was not the answer to getting to Monday. All I had to do was work out what was.

CHAPTER NINETEEN

The next day arrived exactly as before.

Burnt toast.

Smoke alarm.

Dog walk.

TV awards.

Pizza.

I went through the motions in a bit of a daze and by the time we got to Pizza Palace, Dad had picked up that I wasn't myself. I watched the chefs spinning the pizza dough around, doing exactly what they had done each time I'd been there.

"You're terribly quiet, Cory," said Dad. "Is everything OK?"

"I'm just tired," I said.

A little later, while Dad was on the phone to Sydney

talking about opening the public toilets, I stared around the restaurant. I watched the same faces eating the same food and saying the same things. I looked over at Agatha, sitting with her dad and little sister. Agatha was wearing a blue T-shirt which said "WHALES NEED FRIENDS" on the front in big white letters. Her little sister was sitting on her dad's lap, chewing the pizza crust. As before, they were coming to the end of their meal and Agatha was scooping a spoonful of ice cream from a tall chocolate sundae. On the top of the ice cream was a little green paper umbrella.

I lifted a triangle of pizza, ready to take a bite, then stopped. My mouth hung open and the pizza dangled in front of me as I stared at Agatha.

Something was different.

Agatha spotted me staring and frowned at me, then looked away, dipping her spoon back into her ice cream sundae.

Dad put his phone down and must have noticed my dazed expression.

"Is everything all right, Cory?"

I dropped my pizza on to my plate and pushed my chair back, standing up.

"I'll … I'll be back in a bit," I said. I quickly manoeuvred around two waiters carrying trays of drinks and pizzas and arrived at Agatha's table.

"Hi!" I said, loudly. Agatha scowled. Her little sister giggled and waved her pizza crust at me. Her face was smeared with tomato sauce.

"Hello there," said Agatha's dad. He looked at me and then at Agatha, waiting for her to introduce me. She didn't.

"I see you've picked the chocolate sundae, Agatha. Nice, is it?" I said.

Agatha licked her spoon.

"Um, yes. It's really nice," she said. "Is there a problem?"

"No … I just thought you'd be more of a *strawberry sundae* kind of person. You know?"

Agatha froze, the long silver spoon in her mouth. I could feel my heart beating against my ribcage. I was right, I was sure of it! But Agatha just shrugged.

"I fancied chocolate," she said. She carried on eating. Agatha's dad wiped her sister's mouth with a napkin.

"So you're looking out for the whales today," I said, pointing to her top. "I thought you were saving the bees? You know? BEES? Like the ones on your *green* T-shirt?"

Agatha put her spoon down.

"Bees and whales are both vulnerable and they both need our help," she said. "Do you have a problem with that?"

Her dad cleared his throat. "Do you two know each other from school?" he said.

"This is Cory. We're in the same maths class," said Agatha.

"Well, hello, Cory," said her dad. "Are you here on your own?" He glanced around the restaurant. "Because if you are, you're welcome to join us and have something to eat. We can make room."

He began to shuffle his seat to one side.

"No, thank you. I'm just sitting over there with my dad, eating my pizza. AGAIN. And I saw Agatha, AGAIN, and thought I'd come over and say hello." I was watching Agatha when I spoke to see if she reacted to my "agains", but she didn't flinch. There was an awkward silence and then Agatha's dad did a little cough.

"Well, it's been nice to meet you, Cory," said Agatha's dad. "Maybe you'd better get back to your dad in case he's wondering where you are?"

I stood there for a few more seconds. Agatha either had no idea what was going on, or she was very, very good at playing it cool.

"Yeah. I guess so," I said.

"I'll see you at school tomorrow," said Agatha, brightly. And when I looked at her, I could have sworn she was trying not to smirk.

When I got back to our table, Dad had nearly finished his pizza, but I had completely lost my appetite.

"You look a bit pale, Cory," said Dad. "Did something happen over there?"

We both looked over at Agatha who was smiling and behaving as if everything was entirely normal.

"I'm not entirely sure," I said.

When we got home, I went to my room and laid on my bed to think things over. My head was hurting.

I clearly had a choice how to spend the day that I was living. I could decide to wear different clothes, spend a day in bed, save a stuffed dragon from ending up in the pond or get on a bus and travel across town. What was also clear was that everyone else *didn't* have a choice unless I intervened, like when I was "ill" and Dad took Bingo for a walk or when I said something different and they replied in another way. If I didn't interfere, then everyone else continued as before – going to the same places, doing the same things, wearing the same clothes.

Everyone except Agatha.

In the original Sunday and all the other repeated Sundays, I'd seen Agatha in Pizza Palace sitting with her family. She had been wearing a green T-shirt with "SAVE THE BEES" written in yellow lettering. She had also been eating a strawberry sundae – I distinctly remembered seeing the tiny little pink umbrella on the top! But today she was eating a *chocolate* sundae which had a *green* umbrella. And not only that, but she also had on a *blue* T-shirt which said "WHALES NEED FRIENDS" on the front! Agatha was behaving differently. And there was only one explanation.

Agatha was stuck in this Sunday! Just like me!

I jumped up and paced around my room. What should I do? Should I just come right out and ask her? What if she denied it? I was just wondering whether to send her a message from my phone when the doorbell rang. I gasped. *That* had never happened before. I went to my bedroom door and opened it, listening. Dad was talking to someone.

"Oh, hello there. Hang on a minute, I'll just get him. CORY! SOMEONE IS HERE TO SEE YOU!"

I tentatively went to the top of the stairs. I couldn't see who it was from there. My throat felt dry as I made my way down.

"I'll leave you both to it," said Dad. He headed off

to the lounge and I heard the TV go on. I stepped around the door and there, standing on our front step wearing a dark grey hoodie and with a great scowl on her face was Agatha.

"We need to talk," she said.

CHAPTER TWENTY

"Can I come in?" said Agatha.

I moved to one side and she stepped into our hallway and looked around at the boxes of toothpaste we still had piled up.

"We can talk in my room," I said. Agatha followed me upstairs. As soon as she stepped into my room I bombarded her. "You're stuck too! Isn't it unbelievable? What on earth is going on do you think? It's so weird, isn't it? Although kind of lonely too, being the only one reliving everything. Until now that is! I'm so pleased that you—"

Agatha still wasn't smiling and she put her hand up to stop me.

"Look. I only came here to say stay away from me.

It was supposed to be just me here – not me and …
Cory Turner. You are ruining everything!"

"W-what?" I said. "Did you make this happen? But how? Why?"

Agatha shook her head.

"It doesn't matter. What matters is that you stay away from me and my family. OK? This is *my* twenty-four hours and I'm not having you coming along and messing things up."

"What? You *want* to be stuck in one day?" I said.

Agatha took a couple of steps away from me and spotted Bingo curled up on my bed. She went over to him and he sniffed at her hand and wagged his tail. She tickled him behind his ear and he closed his eyes.

I carried on. "I guess it's been OK some of the time. And I am really happy that I don't have to go to school or deal with any of that … rubbish. But if this carries on for much longer, isn't it going to become a bit … boring? And there are people I miss. People I want to see that I can't." I hadn't admitted it to myself yet, but what if I was stuck here for ever? It would mean that I'd never see Mum again! I couldn't bear to think about it.

Agatha turned back to face me.

"My reasons for being here are … personal,"

she said. "You wouldn't understand." I thought she was beginning to look a bit upset. Or maybe I was mistaken and she was just still angry that I was there and "ruining everything".

"You stay in your day, and I'll stay in mine, OK?" she said. Then she held out her hand for me to shake. "Do we have a deal?"

I remembered how I'd seen her on the day I was going to get the train to Scotland and I'd been on the bus to the station. She'd been walking out of the library and had stared at me with an open mouth. It made sense now. She was clearly puzzled about why I was out of sync and in her day, just like she was out of sync in my day eating different food and wearing different clothes at Pizza Palace.

I ignored her hand. Things were getting serious. I mean, I couldn't spend the rest of my life not seeing my own mum, could I?

"But what if I want things to go back to how they were?" I said.

Agatha shook her head and directed her hand towards me again.

"That's not going to happen," she said. "This is it for us now. You can just carry on doing silly childish things like winning the lottery—"

Oh yes! Agatha had been at Pizza Palace when we'd found out the news. That was why she'd been frowning at me. She must have realized I was stuck here too but hadn't said anything!

"You made a choice to be here, Cory. Now shake and let's go our separate ways."

I made a choice? What did that mean?

"Would you just hurry up and shake my hand?" snapped Agatha.

"But I didn't have anything to do with this," I said. "It just happened! The same day keeps playing out over and over and I can't seem to stop it."

Agatha huffed.

"You made a choice. You asked for this to happen!" she said.

"But I didn't!"

Agatha rubbed at her forehead. "You were there on Saturday night, at the Ivy Hill fireworks, yes?"

I nodded.

"And you made a wish, just before the first firework exploded?"

I shook my head. "No! Of course not. I would have remembered if I'd said anything, I—" I stopped.

Agatha folded her arms.

"You did, didn't you? I can tell by your face. What

did you say? You must have said it out loud for it to have worked."

I sat down on my bed and put my head in my hands. "Hang on a minute, I-I need to think."

I went back to that evening. I'd got to the top of the hill and Dad had gone to one of the trailers to get us some hot dogs. Then Rowan overheard Dad talking to me about going to his awards ceremony and me having to miss the football, and Will came over and started winding me up, and then he fell backwards on his bottom. He threatened me and I remember that feeling of despair that he was going to make my life even more miserable at school. The crowd around me had gasped as a rocket launched into the black sky.

That was when I'd said it.

"*I wish Monday would never come,*" I'd whispered. And the rocket had exploded into a purple, twinkling shower of dancing lights.

I put my hands down and looked up at Agatha.

"I did. You're right. I wished that Monday would never come."

"I told you so," said Agatha. "By doing what you did, Monday is never going to arrive. You are going to relive this Sunday for the rest of your life."

"But I didn't mean to do it! I don't want to be stuck any more. Not if it's for ever!"

Agatha shrugged. "Sorry. That's the way it is. So you just keep to your day and I'll keep to mine and we don't need to discuss anything about this ever again. OK?"

She made to leave, and I jumped up off my bed. "No, stop! We need to talk about things. How are we going to get back to normal when we're ready?"

Agatha took a deep breath then let out a long sigh. "We are not going back, Cory. This is it! This is how it's going to be from now on."

I felt tears beginning to prickle my eyes and I quickly blinked them away.

"But … but I don't get it," I said, desperately. "Why would you want to be stuck in the same day? For ever?"

Agatha stared right into my eyes and bit on her bottom lip. "You wouldn't understand," she said.

She walked towards my doorway. "Just keep out of my way, Cory Turner. And don't approach me in Pizza Palace ever again."

She hesitated for a second, then turned and ran down the stairs. The front door opened and clicked closed behind her.

CHAPTER TWENTY-ONE

I woke to the smell of burning toast and put my arm over my eyes.

Beeping smoke alarm.

"Can you take Bingo out for a walk?"

Park.

Angry cyclist.

Jogger.

Arguing couple.

Archie's dragon in the pond.

Boring awards.

Dad loses.

Pizza.

Home.

Sleep.

CHAPTER TWENTY-TWO

I woke to the smell of burning toast.

I did my "I'm-sick-and-can't-go-to-the-awards-ceremony" routine again. It wasn't getting any easier, fibbing to Dad, but this was important. I needed to stay home and work out another plan to get back to Monday.

When Dad left for the awards, I went downstairs to the kitchen and unplugged the toaster. The smell of burning toast was the common thread to every single one of my Sundays. It was the first thing I noticed in the morning. My thinking was, if I removed the toaster then Dad couldn't burn the toast so maybe it would undo the sequence of events and it would be Monday again.

It was worth a try.

Bingo lifted his head and watched me as I stood there, clutching the toaster to my chest, wondering where to put it. If I just stuffed it in a kitchen cupboard there was a danger that Dad might find it and put it back – after asking me why it was there in the first place, of course. I took the key to the shed from the hook by our back door and headed outside. That would be a good place to hide it. The last time I'd been in the shed was about two years ago when I'd tried to find my old pogo stick. But when I opened the door, it looked like Dad had been in there recently. On the wall, by the lawnmower and garden tools, was a cork pinboard that was covered with newspaper cuttings and photos. I took a closer look. In the centre was a black-and-white photograph of Dad when he was younger, standing at the front of a stage with his arms around his fellow actors. It looked like it had been taken at the end of a play when they bowed while everyone clapped. Dad looked really happy. Genuinely happy rather than false, cheesy happy which he seemed to be like now. Beside the photo was a newspaper article giving this production of *Hamlet* a three-star review. I spotted Dad's name in the final paragraph.

Even though this was a mediocre interpretation of Hamlet *at best, special note must be made of promising young actor, Dennis Turner, who stole the scene as the Gravedigger. I suspect this young man will go far.*

I looked at the other pictures. There were more of Dad on stage, one of him dressed in a khaki soldier's uniform and one with him dressed as a king, sitting on a throne. I spotted some five-star reviews and all of them mentioned Dad and his "unquestionable talent". Dad really *was* good at acting then? There were also a couple taken on the set of the TV soap, *Albany Road*. These photos were coloured and glossy and Dad seemed to be in the middle of acting in a couple of them, waving his fist at a man and sitting on a sofa and crying in another. I spotted a photo of Mum on the set too so these must have dated back to when they met. Amongst the newspaper clippings were some family photos. There was one of me when I was three, sitting in front of a big birthday cake in the shape of a yellow bus. I was about to blow out the candles and my cheeks were inflated with air and my eyes were bulging. There was another one of me standing on our front doorstep wearing a school uniform, taken on my very first day of school. I guessed that *I* was part of Dad's achievements too. It wasn't just the fame or the TV that made him feel good about himself. I made him proud too. I unpinned a strip of four square photos that we had had taken in a photo booth at the seaside about four years ago. We'd decided to pull silly faces and in the last picture our faces were screwed up with hysterical laughter. That had been a good day. Seeing Mum made my chest tighten. Was I ever going to see her again?

I took a long breath and pinned it back on the board. Then I got back to the job in hand and looked around for somewhere to put the toaster. In a corner was a metal filing cabinet with two drawers. I opened one. It was filled with files labelled things like "Contracts" and "Scripts". I could probably squeeze the toaster in there so I pushed some of the files back to make room. On the bottom of the drawer was a postcard. The picture on the front was of the famous Hollywood sign. I picked it up and turned it over. It was addressed to Dad.

Dennis! There is a director here who is really keen to meet you about a movie he's making. He saw you in Albany Road and said that he's got a part for you! Can you get a flight next week?

You can stay with me! Filming starts in six weeks and you'd be here for at least another three months I'd think. What do you say? Fancy a bit of the Hollywood life?! Martin.

WHAT?! Dad had the chance to go to HOLLYWOOD?! And be in a movie? I was stunned! Did Mum even know about this? The date on the postcard was not long after I'd been born. Why hadn't he gone? Did it have something to do with me? I put the postcard back where I'd found it and closed the drawer. I found a hiding place for the toaster – inside an old bucket, covered with a dust sheet – but all I could think about was how Dad had been invited to meet a Hollywood director! The date of the postcard was three months after I was born and, as far as I know, he didn't go.

I went back indoors, ate some biscuits and put a film on, though I couldn't concentrate on it. I just kept thinking about Dad and why he hadn't jumped at the chance to be in a Hollywood movie.

Dad arrived back from the awards and came in and sat on the sofa. He looked tired.

"How are you feeling now, Cory?"

"Better, thanks." I studied his face. He seemed different now. More serious.

"I didn't win, I'm afraid," he said.

"Sorry, Dad." He patted my knee.

We watched the TV in silence for a while.

"Dad? Have you ever had the chance to go to Hollywood? Like Martin has?"

I wanted to see what he'd say, if he'd open up about why he turned down the chance all those years ago.

Dad rubbed his face with his hand and took a long breath.

"There was this one time. It was years ago now, but apparently some hotshot director wanted to give me a part in his movie. Me? Can you imagine it!" He smiled.

"That's amazing, Dad! Why didn't you go?"

Dad picked at one of the sequins on his trousers. "You know, Cory. Sometimes you have to make decisions that might not seem to be the most sensible, but in the end they're the best decision for you *and* the people around you."

"What do you mean?"

"I mean that the invitation to go to America came at the wrong time in my life. So I had to say no."

I swallowed. "Were you asked … when I'd just been born?"

Dad looked at me and frowned. "Well, yes. It wasn't that long after, actually. And there was no way

I was going to miss your first few weeks. Your mum and I were so thrilled to have you."

I stayed silent. It kind of felt like it was my fault he didn't go. If I hadn't have been born, maybe Dad would be a movie star.

"I'm sorry, Dad," I said. "I'm sorry you missed your chance because of me."

Dad spun round on the sofa. "You don't ever need to say sorry, Cory! Not for one second. I made a decision and it was the best decision of my life. And do you know why?"

I shook my head and he reached his arm towards me and grabbed my hand.

"Because I got to spend precious time with you and Mum in those first few weeks. And you two are the best thing that has ever happened to me. Back then I couldn't contemplate spending months away from home. It wasn't an option!"

My head was reeling with all of this information.

"You were good at acting, weren't you? You could have stayed on the soap and acted for ever. You could have starred in films like Martin!"

Dad shrugged. "Maybe. Who knows. But anyway, that's all in the past now. And remember that I am incredibly lucky. I've just been nominated for an award, remember! You can't knock that, can you? Right. I'm going to make some tea."

He got up and I stared at the TV. I'd never seen this side of Dad before. I knew he loved us, but I always thought he put himself first. But that was clearly not the case.

Dad didn't notice that the toaster was missing and when I went to bed I had one more thing to try. I took the batteries out of my alarm clock.

No toaster – no burnt toast.

No batteries – no alarm clock saying a later time.

I closed my eyes and crossed my fingers.

This was going to work, wasn't it?

CHAPTER
TWENTY-THREE

I woke to the smell of burning toast.

"NOT AGAIN!" I shouted out loud.

My clock was beside me, the batteries back in the compartment. The time read 7.58 a.m.

Considering I could smell burnt toast, I could only assume that the toaster had somehow magically returned to the kitchen counter too.

A tightness squeezed my chest as the smoke alarm began to beep.

I couldn't do this any more. I couldn't keep reliving the same day over and over and over. And Agatha had the answer – I knew it. Maybe if I could work out *why* she had chosen to live stuck in the same day for all eternity, then I could work on persuading her to help me get back to normality. She seemed to get on OK at school. I never heard kids yelling at her in the corridor or saw her being told off by the teachers. In fact, apart from being in the bottom set for maths like me, she seemed to sail through school! What problem did she have with Monday that was so bad she was willing to live the rest of her life in a never-ending Sunday?

There was only one way to find out. I had to follow her and discover what it was that she was avoiding. I didn't know where she lived, but I did know where she'd be in approximately two hours' time. Outside the town library. That's if her day took the same pattern that it had before. If not, then I'd just have to follow her from Pizza Palace, but I hoped it wouldn't come to that.

Dad came upstairs and asked me to take Bingo for a walk, and I told him I didn't feel well. I had done this so many times now that remembering to sound genuine was becoming harder.

"Are you sure, Cory? You don't look ill," said Dad.

I nodded. "I'm sorry, Dad. I really wanted to be there for you today."

After a bit more acting from me, he seemed convinced and took Bingo for his walk and not long after, was on his way to the awards. As soon as I heard the car *POP* and reverse off our driveway I jumped out of bed.

The town library was only one bus stop away so I decided to walk there. I passed two women who were talking about going to see a film that night at the cinema, then a ginger and white cat walked along beside me on a garden wall. I stopped to stroke him and he brushed up against my side. When I walked away he sat watching me, his tail swishing.

I went past the bench where the angry cyclist was sitting, his bike propped beside him. When I got closer, I realized he was out of breath and his face was wet with sweat. He looked down at his open satchel. Inside I could see a small black purse with a gold emblem on the front. He glanced up at me and quickly folded over the top of the bag.

I carried on. Outside the newsagent's was an old man wearing a suit and tie with a navy baseball cap. He had a collection tin for a mental health charity. The suit looked rather big and I guessed it might not have always belonged to him. He shook the tin which gave a feeble rattle.

"Any donations," he said. "Any donations."

I stopped and took my wallet out of my pocket. I knew that I had a twenty-pound note inside which had been in there since my birthday. I had been planning on buying myself a second-hand computer game from our local gaming exchange shop, but there didn't seem to be any point now – unless I kept going back every day to re-buy it. I folded the note and slotted it into the tiny hole in the top of his collection tin.

"Why, thank you. That is incredibly generous of you," said the man. He tipped his baseball cap and gave me a big smile. I nodded and carried on. It felt nice doing something good, but I knew it wouldn't last. At midnight tonight the twenty-pound note would vanish from the box as if it had never been in there and the man would be back here tomorrow, rattling the tin, asking for "any donations".

I got to the library and hurried up the slope to see if Agatha was inside. The automatic doors whooshed open and I went in. There was a sign that said:

IVY HILL EXHIBITION

Next to it was an arrow pointing to the stairs. I remembered something our form tutor, Ms Horne, had said last week. She'd told us that the library had a new display of local history and that we should all go and see it. I saw someone out of the corner of my eye. It was Agatha. She was using the computer screen to check out some books. I ducked behind a stand of leaflets and grabbed one, shielding my face. She walked past me, the books in her arms, and the doors whooshed open again and she was off.

I kept a few paces behind her as she headed further into town. She went into a clothes shop and I watched through the window as she flicked through the rails of clothes. She picked out a pale pink jumper, then a silver-grey scarf and went to the counter to pay. Is this why she didn't want to go back? So that she could spend her days shopping and buying things she wanted? Wasn't that a bit sad? I ducked into a shop doorway as she came out and then she was off again. She came to a stop outside a busy coffee shop and went inside. I watched as she went to the counter, a big smile on her face, and then came out carrying a large hot chocolate with whipped cream and marshmallow sprinkles. Now *that* was a good idea. I had the feeling that Agatha had probably nailed the whole "repeating-day" routine. From here it looked like she was quite enjoying herself by buying things she'd never need to pay for. Why hadn't I thought of that?

Her pace slowed and every now and then she stopped to take a slurp of her drink. I followed her around the edge of the market square. There was some kind of commotion going on in the middle of the stalls and Agatha paused for a moment and then she looked up. I followed her gaze. There was a big bunch of helium balloons floating across the sky! I could make out a large purple unicorn's head and a yellow daisy. The seller must have let go of them. Agatha shook her head and carried on. She popped into a few more shops and it was all getting a bit boring, but then she turned down a side road and began to head away from the centre of town. I guessed she was walking home.

It was harder to be incognito now as there were only the two of us on the street. I followed her across a few roads, then she turned left and right, then stopped to get a key out of her pocket. We were outside a small, detached bungalow with lavender bushes along a front wall. I hung back and watched as she unlocked the door and went in.

I still had no idea why she was so keen for time not to move on, but I couldn't exactly ring the doorbell and ask. Especially when she'd been so angry with me yesterday. Maybe she just wanted to spend the rest of her life borrowing library books she'd never have time to read, buying jumpers and scarves and drinking hot chocolate? I walked up the pathway to the front of the bungalow. On the left-hand side was a skinny alleyway which I guessed led to the back garden.

I hesitated for a moment, then, before I changed my mind, I darted around the side, past three wheelie bins and up to a tall wooden gate. I lifted the latch as quietly as I could, then pushed the gate and emerged into a pretty garden. There were stepping stones running through the middle of a lawn and a pond with a trickling fountain. I was just going to see if I could look through one of the windows when the back door opened and out came Agatha. In her hand was the shopping bag from earlier. The one with the pale pink jumper and scarf. She skipped along the stepping stones towards a wide old apple tree. There was someone there, sitting in a chair in the dappled shade. It was a woman. She was wearing a roll-neck soft, white jumper and jogging bottoms. Around her head was a multicoloured scarf. I quickly shot across the patio and crouched behind a circular shaped bush.

"Hi, Mum! I got your library books. I've left them

inside. I got you a present too."

Agatha opened the bag and pulled out the jumper.

"Oh, Agatha. You didn't need to get me anything," said her mum. She was smiling. She looked tired and there was something different about her face, but I couldn't place exactly what it was.

"I thought the colour would suit you," said Agatha. She held it up against her mum and then nodded. "Yep. You are going to look amazing in that."

Her mum laughed and put her hand to her head. "We'll see," she said.

"I thought you might want to try a different scarf too," said Agatha. "It might go better with the pink." She pulled out the soft grey scarf and unravelled it. Dots of sunlight landed on the scarf creating a dancing pattern.

"Oh, that is beautiful," said her mum. "It's such a lovely colour. Thank you, darling."

"Try it on!" said Agatha.

Her mum put her hands to the back of her head and unknotted the scarf, letting it fall on to her lap.

I'd seen someone looking like Agatha's mum before. My Uncle Jim. The treatment he'd had had made him lose all of his hair as well and that included his eyelashes and his eyebrows too.

Agatha's mum folded the scarf, then held it against her forehead and tied it neatly at the back. The colour made her eyes the brightest blue.

"How does it look?" she said. Agatha gave her a kiss on the cheek, and knelt down at her feet, resting her arms on her mum's lap.

"You look incredible," she said. "How are you feeling now?"

"I'm feeling better every day," said her mum, stroking her daughter's hair. "You mustn't keep worrying. Everything is going to be OK."

It felt wrong to be watching. This was a private moment between a mum and daughter, and I shouldn't be there. I slowly edged my way backwards into the alleyway and carefully lifted the latch on the wooden gate. I walked through, closed the gate and stood there for a moment as everything began to fall into place.

Now it made sense why Agatha didn't want Monday to arrive. Now I knew why she wanted to stay in the same day, repeating it over and over and over. Her mum was sick. Seriously sick. And she wanted to have her for ever.

CHAPTER
TWENTY-FOUR

I slowly made my way home.

It must be so difficult for Agatha to see her mum going through so much. Frightening too. I wasn't sure how I would have coped if it was me seeing Mum or Dad like that. But I wasn't sure that living trapped in one day was the right thing to do, either. I had to persuade Agatha that this couldn't carry on – that we needed to work out how to reverse whatever it was that had happened to us.

I made myself some beans on toast, then went to my room. Dad would be home and expecting to see me in my sick bed soon. Lying about being ill felt even more wrong now.

I picked up my phone, ready to compose a message

to Agatha who I estimated was probably in Pizza Palace right now, tucking into a strawberry sundae, or maybe it was going to be a banana split this time?

I decided it would probably be easier to explain everything in person. This was a delicate situation, after all. I tapped on the screen.

Hi Agatha, it's Cory. We need to talk.

I waited for her to answer but my phone remained silent. She was ignoring me.

Dad came home from the awards, looking sad behind his smile.

"I didn't win," he said, sitting at the end of my bed.

"I'm sorry," I said.

Dad sighed, his head hanging down.

I thought about the missed opportunities he'd had. Maybe he still had another chance?

"Dad? Have you ever thought about finding some auditions yourself?" I asked.

Dad looked up. "What do you mean? Behind Sydney's back?"

"Yes! She's not exactly your biggest fan, is she?"

Dad looked confused.

"No. I can't do that. Besides, I'll be filming more

episodes of *Déjà Vu* in a few weeks."

Of course! He didn't know that Timothy Gosling would be taking over his job. Not yet anyway.

"Things move quickly in the entertainment world. You've said that yourself before! So, say you found yourself *without* a presenting job, then it wouldn't do any harm to … have a plan B. How about going back to the theatre? You loved that, didn't you?"

Dad looked even more forlorn then. "I don't think so, Cory. I've missed the boat on that one. And Sydney doesn't think I'm good enough."

I'd never heard Dad sound dejected like this. But I knew a lot about Sydney now and the main thing I'd learnt was that she was completely untrustworthy and a liar. I believed Dad was a good actor. Those newspaper cuttings in the shed proved it! He just needed to find a new agent who really believed in him, and that would get his confidence back. He wouldn't leave Sydney, but maybe he could do something else to make him feel better.

"How about Boxwick Theatre? There's a poster on the wall for auditions! Why don't you find out about them?"

Dad perked up a little. But then his shoulders

dropped a little. "Sydney wouldn't agree to that. Even if I got a part there's no fee as it'll be an amateur production."

I sat forward. "But does that matter? Why not audition and just see how you get on? You'll be doing something you love and who knows where it might lead!"

Dad had a soft smile on his face and he did seem to be thinking seriously about the idea. But then he slapped his hands against the tops of his thighs and stood up.

"It's a nice idea, Cory. But I couldn't possibly do it around all the filming I have coming up. Thank you for thinking of me though." He reached out a hand and ruffled my hair.

"Right, I'd better go and feed Bingo. I'll be up to check on you in a bit."

I sighed as I heard him head downstairs. Convincing Dad to try and audition was pointless anyway. Even if he agreed we'd just be back to square one tomorrow. This whole thing was beginning to feel like a repeating nightmare. I checked my phone and saw that Agatha was typing.

I told you not to approach me ever again.

I grinned.

> No you didn't. You said not to approach you
> in Pizza Palace again. And I'm not in Pizza
> Palace. :)

I waited but she didn't start typing. So I sent another message.

> We need to talk. About your mum.

I waited a little longer, and then I sent another.

> I'm sorry. It must be difficult for you.

There was a brief pause and then her answer popped up on my screen.

> Meet me by the cafe in the park tomorrow
> morning at nine.

That night I went to bed with my heart feeling a little lighter. I was sure that between Agatha and me, we could work out how to get back to Monday.

The next morning, I headed to the park with

Bingo. I left a bit earlier and walked in the direction from where the dangerous cyclist came from.

"I know he's up to something," I said to Bingo, who was pulling in the other direction, trying to get back to the park.

I looked down the road. There was a woman pushing a buggy. She had a bag on her arm and her ear pressed against a phone on her shoulder. Pedalling up behind her was the boy. He bounced his bike up the kerb, then as he passed her he reached into her bag and grabbed her purse. As he hurtled towards me, he unflapped the top of his satchel and dropped the purse inside.

"Stop!" yelled the woman. I didn't know what to do. I held up my arms and waved them at the cyclist, blocking his way, but he just jumped off the kerb, biked around me and in through the park gates. Another woman must have heard the commotion and came running out of her house. She hurried over to the woman with the buggy.

"I knew it! He's a thief!," I said to Bingo. The woman with the buggy looked shaken but OK, and the other woman had her arm around her. I checked my watch. It was nearly nine a.m.

"We'd better get going, Bingo."

I spotted Agatha leaning against the cafe wall eating an apple. She looked relaxed, as if she didn't have a care in the world.

"Hi," I said. Bingo trotted up to her, wagging his tail madly. She bent down and tickled him between his ears. "Hello, little guy," she said. "You're rather cute, aren't you?"

Over Agatha's shoulder I spied Caroline and Wayne sitting in silence with their hot drinks. Any minute now they'd start arguing. There'd be no proposal in this version of today.

"Shall we move? Those two are going to have a row in a bit." I nodded towards the couple.

Agatha shrugged. "Sure," she said. It was nice to talk to someone who wasn't shocked by the fact that I knew what was going to happen next.

Bingo began to pull on his lead. The smell of ducks in the air was too much for him to ignore and we followed him towards the pond. Little Archie was there, clutching his dragon.

"I've been thinking of ways that we might get back to normal. Maybe all of this is happening because of my dad's TV show? *Déjà Vu*? I mean, we are stuck in one massive version of *Déjà Vu* when you think about it," I said. "Could that be it?"

Agatha spluttered. "Erm, I don't think so," she said. We watched as the woman in the yellow coat threw the pellets for the ducks. The quacking noise increased with each handful.

"OK, so maybe it's not the TV show then," I said. "Do you have any idea how we get back to Monday?"

Agatha folded her arms.

"You don't get to say what happens," she said. "It's not up to you."

The woman in the yellow coat was telling Archie to "look at the ducks" again so I knew what was coming.

"Hang on a minute," I said. I stepped forward as Archie swung his arm and threw the dragon into the air. I caught it and casually handed it back. The family stared at me, open mouthed.

I saw a flicker of a smile on Agatha's mouth.

"I see you've found ways of helping then?" she said. "Feels good, doesn't it? I've got a little schedule myself. Which reminds me..." She checked her watch. "I need to stop a woman walking into a lamp post outside the cinema in twenty minutes."

Archie was staring up at me like I was some kind of superhero again. This time it was making me feel a bit uncomfortable.

"Come on, let's keep walking," I said. I knew that

Will and Rowan would be coming from the other direction any minute now and I really didn't want to see them, so I led us towards a bench, close to the playground. I scooped Bingo on to my lap then checked my watch. I couldn't be much longer, or Dad would be ringing asking where I was.

"Look, Agatha. I know why you don't want this day to end. Your mum is sick, isn't she? Is it cancer?"

Agatha stared down at the ground.

"How do you know?"

I felt quite awkward about this bit.

"I followed you," I said.

Agatha twisted around to face me. "You did what?"

"I'm sorry! I was desperate! I want things to go back to how they were. And I couldn't understand why you wanted to stay here so much. But now it makes sense."

She turned back and took a breath.

"I'm so sorry, Agatha. But you can't stop your own life because of what's happened to your mum," I said.

She glared at me. "Can't I? How would you feel if it was one of your parents? Do you know how agonizing it is not knowing if the treatment has worked or not?"

She was right, of course. I didn't know how that felt. I could only imagine how awful it must be.

"Has she finished her treatment?"

Agatha nodded. "She's due to go to hospital tomorrow to get her results to see if it's worked or not. If tomorrow ever comes, that is. Which it won't. Which means she'll always be fine."

"But she might be OK!" I said. "The results could be good, and reliving the day is just a waste of time for everyone!"

Agatha shook her head.

"I can't take that chance. The Ivy Hill fireworks only come around once a year. If the results are bad, I'd have to wait another year to relive a day. And a year is a long time when you're sick."

This was becoming one of the hardest conversations I'd ever had. I understood why Agatha was feeling like this. She was scared. I got it. But this was no way to live. We sat in silence for a while and then I swallowed and turned to face her slightly.

"What about your little sister?"

Agatha looked puzzled. "Maggie? What about her?"

"Maggie will never get the chance to grow up. She'll always be trapped in a toddler's body doing toddler stuff. Is that fair? What about *her* life?"

Agatha frowned. "Maggie is fine," she said. "She's happy."

"What about going to school? Reading a book on

her own? Learning how to ride a bike, to swim, to build a snowman? She'll never get those moments."

Agatha didn't say anything and chewed at the side of her cheek. There was something else that I needed to say.

"And … if we don't go back, well, I won't see my mum again. She's away this weekend, working in Madrid. I've got no way of getting there or telling her to come home." I felt tears spring to my eyes. "I've lost her if this carries on."

Agatha swallowed, looking down at the ground. Then she reached a hand out and squeezed my arm.

"I'm sorry, Cory," she said. "I really am." Then she got up and hurried in the opposite direction.

I didn't see Agatha at Pizza Palace that night. The table where her family usually sat was empty. I guessed she'd directed them somewhere else, or maybe she had told a white lie and said she didn't feel up to going.

I sent her a few messages, begging her to reconsider. I was convinced she would know how to reverse what had happened, whereas I had no clue whatsoever. But Agatha didn't answer.

That night, I grabbed my mobile phone to send

a message. It was really late now and I wasn't sure if she'd read it before the day ended. If she didn't and the day repeated itself again, then she'd never see it. But I typed, anyway.

I love you, Mum. x

I hit send, put the phone on my bedside table, then rolled over and curled myself up into a ball, waiting for sleep to come.

CHAPTER
TWENTY-FIVE

I woke to the smell of burning toast.

The clock beside my bed read 7.58 a.m.

The smoke alarm began to beep.

I bit my lip as I checked my phone. There was no text from Mum. Even if she'd replied while I'd been asleep, everything would have reset, and I'd never get to see her message anyway.

I put my face into my pillow and began to cry. At first it felt horrible. I mean, who likes crying? But after a few seconds I started to feel a sense of relief. With each sob I was beginning to let go of stuff: the anger I felt towards Agatha, the sadness of not being able to see Mum or explain anything to Dad, my upset for Dad missing out on his chance to be a successful actor and being conned by Sydney, the worry I'd been carrying for so long about struggling with maths and all the cruel things Will had said over the past few weeks. And then of course, losing my best friend Rowan. We used to tell each other everything! If we had been getting on better I probably would have gone to his house and asked him for help. All of this came out of me in a huge, soggy, wet mess on to my pillowcase. After a while, I stopped. I sat up, sniffing. I felt a bit better, my shoulders a bit lighter. Crying was weird like that. It kind of made you feel a bit better at the end.

I could hear Dad coming up the stairs to ask me to take Bingo out and I quickly called to him.

"Don't come in! I'm getting dressed!"

"OK, Cory. Can you take Bingo out?" he said from behind the door. "And when you get back you'd better have a shower and get ready. Time is pushing on."

I heard him thump back down the stairs.

My phone buzzed and I quickly grabbed it. It was a text from Agatha.

I've been thinking about what you said.

There was a pause as she wrote another message.

You're right. We need to get back to normality.

I couldn't believe it! She was agreeing with me! I quickly typed a reply.

Thank you! Thank you so much!

My heart was pounding. This was the best news ever! We were going to get back to Monday! I wrote another message.

So, how do we do it? How do we get back?

I waited. It took a few seconds but then Agatha began to type and when I read her message, my heart sank to the soles of my feet.

I have no idea.

We arranged to meet in the park again and I spotted her, leaning up against a wall outside the cafe. She was wearing her "SAVE THE BEES" T-shirt with joggers and trainers. Bingo was walking too slowly so I picked him up.

"What do you mean you have no idea?" I said,

storming up to her. "You must know how to get back. It's your fault we're here in the first place!"

"No, it isn't. I already told you. You did this yourself, not me," said Agatha, pushing herself away from the wall.

Caroline and Wayne looked over at us and I realized that we must have been shouting.

"Come on," I said. "Let's go for a walk."

We headed to a small, grassy slope and sat down. I put Bingo on my lap and he panted as he looked around. A gentle breeze made his ears flap and he sniffed into the air.

"What made you change your mind?" I asked.

Agatha twisted a strand of her hair, then tucked it behind her ear.

"Maggie," she said. "You were right. My little sister needs to be able to grow up and I'm stopping her from doing that."

I nodded.

"And you will get to see your mum again," she continued. "It's not fair that you can't."

I was pleased she understood. "Thank you. I know it's hard, but you've made the right decision."

Agatha stared down at her joggers and picked at a thread.

"The way I understand it is that we got here because we made a wish on Ivy Hill. Even though I did it accidentally," I said.

Agatha nodded.

"So in that case let's just go back to the hill and make another wish. I wish Monday comes. Something like that?"

Agatha rolled her eyes.

"You can't just get your wish on any day. The whole point is that you make them on the anniversary of when Ivy saved the town. It only works on one day of the year."

I felt a tightness in my chest. This was very, very worrying. "But that day won't arrive for us ever again," I said. "Not if we are trapped here where it's always Sunday."

Agatha began to look concerned then, which freaked me out even more. If she couldn't get us back, who could?

She frowned and began to chew on the edge of her thumb. Then she seemed to shake the worry away and got serious.

"The worst thing we can do is panic," she said. "We have time to work it out after all. Have you tried anything so far to reverse what's happened?"

I sat up a little straighter.

"Yes. I put our toaster in the garden shed," I said, with all the seriousness of a detective inspector.

Agatha's forehead creased, and then she appeared to be trying not to laugh. "You put the toaster in the shed? Why? Do you think it's got some kind of magical power or something?"

"No! Nothing like that. Every morning, Dad burns his toast. I thought if there was no toaster then it might, I don't know, unsettle the pattern or something. I tried taking the batteries out of my alarm clock too. Nothing worked."

Agatha smirked and put a hand to her mouth, clearly finding my attempts highly amusing.

"Oh, I'm sorry I'm not an expert on how to reset a blip in the whole time and space quantum physics and whatnot," I said, huffing loudly. Agatha seemed to find that even funnier. She patted Bingo on his back.

"I'm sorry. I'm not teasing you. I just think it might take more than ... moving a toaster ... to get us back, that's all," she said through her giggles.

I waited until she'd stop laughing.

"Well, go on then, you come up with something if you're so smart!" I said. "We can't wish ourselves back. We can't reset the start of the day. What else is there?"

Agatha had composed herself now.

"Have you tried staying up past midnight?" she asked.

I shook my head. "Have you?" That was a good one.

"Yes. But I was in bed and I must have fallen asleep because the next thing I knew I was waking up as usual. Oh, by the way, you're really lucky your day starts with just the smell of burnt toast! The start to my day is nowhere near as relaxing."

"What happens in your morning?" I asked.

Agatha rolled her eyes. "As soon as I wake up I hear Maggie singing, *'The horn on the bus goes beep, beep, beep'* at the top of her voice. It was cute the first time. Now, not so much."

I could imagine. Burnt toast was much easier to deal with.

"That must be awful."

"Just a bit," said Agatha. She plucked a few blades of grass. "I wanted to ask something, Cory. You know why I didn't want Monday to come, but why didn't you?"

I felt warmth spread across my cheeks. My reasons for not wanting Monday to arrive felt small compared to Agatha's worries about losing her mum.

"Am I right in thinking it has something to do with that boy over there? Will Higgs?" Will and Rowan were now walking along the pathway, heading to the football. Will with his arm in a sling. The sight of them still made my stomach do a little somersault. If Monday arrived, I'd have to face all of that again.

"Will Higgs hates me. And he's blaming me for hurting his arm, which isn't true, and he said he's going to get me in trouble. And because everyone loves him, I've got no chance."

Agatha watched them. They were chatting and laughing together.

"I know. It sounds a bit rubbish compared to you … you know. Your mum," I said, feeling a little uncomfortable.

But Agatha didn't seem to mind. "It's horrible when you have something worrying you. Whatever it might be."

Will and Rowan went out of sight, Rowan laughing at something Will had just said.

"I know. Let's meet tonight and we try to stay up past midnight."

I smiled. That would be easy enough to do.

"Great," I said.

"Bring anything you can to help keep us awake," said Agatha. "Can you get out around nine p.m.?"

"Yes. Where shall we meet?" I didn't fancy wandering around town late at night. And the park gates were locked at eight p.m.

"Meet me at the bus stop at the end of your road and we can walk to Ivy Hill together. It makes sense to go where it all started, I guess."

Agatha stood and I got Bingo off my lap. He gave himself a shake and Agatha put her fingers in between Bingo's ears and ruffled his fur. He lifted his head, his eyes closed with the bliss of being tickled.

"What are you going to do for the rest of the day?" I asked, getting up.

Agatha carried on stroking my dog. "I always try to do something nice for my mum. I usually get her some books from the library and buy her a scarf I know she'll like. Or maybe I'll get her a necklace this time. Then of course we have pizza tonight. Which reminds me. Sometimes you're not there? How come?"

"We have to go to this really long and boring ceremony because my dad is nominated for an award. Sometimes I can't face it and say I'm unwell and I stay at home, watching telly mostly. Although once I tried to get a train to Scotland to see if that broke the spell. But that didn't work out. A bit like the toaster, I guess."

Agatha smiled and I was grateful she didn't seem to be judging me for lying to my dad.

"That's cool about your dad's nomination. Does he win?"

I shook my head. Did she just say the word "cool" in a sentence about my dad?

"You must be really proud of him. I would be," said Agatha.

"Um, yes. I guess so. But I've not been so good at showing it," I muttered.

"Right. I'd better get going. I'll see you tonight, Cory. Nine p.m. At the bus stop. Don't be late!"

I felt a huge wave of relief as I watched her walk away towards the cafe. I didn't have to do this on my own any more. And not only that, we had a plan.

CHAPTER TWENTY-SIX

I managed to sit through the awards ceremony without falling asleep and when I saw Agatha in Pizza Palace she gave me a wave and a big smile.

When we got home, I went to my room and listened to Dad boiling the kettle to make his chamomile tea and then my phone began to ping with the flurry of messages on the group chat. The one where Will had kicked off about me hurting his arm.

Did you hear what Showbiz Smile Jr did to me at the fireworks? Cory is going to be in so much trouble tomorrow.

The messages continued as they always did, until there was one by someone who hadn't joined in before. Agatha.

Interesting fact! Did you know that one of
the reasons someone is a bully is because
they feel insignificant in their own life. Do
you want to talk, Will?

I couldn't believe she'd said that! I waited, watching the screen to see if someone was going to say something but everyone remained silent. Then I saw Will was writing.

Shut up, Agatha.

Ha! That was a pathetic response! Agatha 1, Will 0. I grinned and then deleted the messages. Maybe if Monday arrived he'd think a bit differently about how he spoke to me.

It wasn't long until Dad came upstairs and went into the bathroom. I heard the shower turn on and I jumped out of bed. I knew he wouldn't come into my room so I was free to leave. I put my hoodie on, then snuck downstairs. Agatha had said something about bringing stuff to keep us awake. I knew coffee had caffeine which kept you awake but I didn't like that. Sugar did too, didn't it? I grabbed the pack of custard creams and found two bags of giant jelly babies in the cupboard. I put them in a carrier bag, then quietly slipped out of the front door.

Agatha was standing under the shelter wearing a black puffer coat with a bag under her arm. She looked like she was just waiting for a bus.

"All set?" she said.

"Yep. Let's do this," I said.

We began to walk. The air felt fresher at this time of night and I wished I'd put a coat on like Agatha had.

"Thanks for what you said on the group chat. To Will," I said.

"No worries." Agatha put her hands into her coat pockets.

"Do you know, I think you're the only other person who realizes Will's not very nice."

Agatha snorted. "I doubt it. I'm sure lots of other people don't like him, but they don't want to say anything or they'll stand out and end up being a target too."

I thought of Rowan. He must realize Will wasn't very nice to me. But it was easier for him to just stand back and do nothing. I wasn't sure I really wanted a friend like that.

"And what I said to him was true," continued Agatha. "He just picks on you to make up for whatever is wrong in his life."

"Do you really think so?"

I glanced at her and she nodded. "I know so. You know he wins all those swimming trophies all the time? Well, big shocker coming – Will Higgs hates swimming. He only goes because his dad makes him."

I was stunned. Will hates swimming? I thought of how often he'd boasted about being in the pool at half past five in the morning before school each day.

"How do you know that?" I said.

"My dad used to work at the leisure centre and I heard him talking to Mum when they didn't know I was listening. He said he saw Will's dad practically dragging him through the leisure centre door each morning. He didn't want to be there. It's his dad who makes him go and pushes him so much."

"That's actually quite sad," I said.

"Yep. I think he only boasts about his swimming to take away from the fact he doesn't actually enjoy it or really want to do it."

My parents had never done anything like that with me. We got to the path that led to Ivy Hill and made our way up.

"But he acts so big and confident all the time. He's *really* got it in for my dad too. He can be so nasty sometimes."

"He's probably jealous of you," said Agatha. I stopped in my tracks. Jealous? Why on earth would Will Higgs be jealous of me? Agatha kept walking and I hurried to catch her up.

"What do you mean?" I said.

"I bet he's envious of your dad and he's deflecting that feeling by constantly being rude about him."

I almost wanted to laugh. Who would want my dad as their father? He's a laughing stock.

Will's dad probably had a proper job and didn't wear suits with sequins all over them. As the hill got steeper, we put our heads down and pressed on. When we got to the top, Agatha sat on the grass and leaned back on her elbows. I sat down beside her.

"I'm sorry, Agatha, but I can't believe Will is jealous of my dad. Have you seen him recently? He's orange!"

Agatha sighed. "Think about it, Cory. Will's dad makes him do swimming, which he doesn't want to do. So he's probably breathing down his neck about other stuff too. Being school captain, getting the best grades. All that pressure! Whereas your dad isn't like

242

that. He's fun. He's always happy and he's friendly. Everyone thinks he's nice."

I frowned. "Do you think so?"

"Yes!" said Agatha. "Take it from me. Will picks on you because he wishes he had a dad like yours. He probably made up the damaged arm to get out of swimming too. And it was easy to blame you for it."

He *had* told me he wasn't going to be able to compete in the county championships because of his injury. But Agatha was making it sound like he didn't want to do it in the first place!

Agatha lay back and stared up at the dark sky. I did the same, taking in everything she'd just said. It was starting to make a lot of sense.

"Right," she said. "Did you bring any supplies? I've got two cans of Coca-Cola."

I presented the custard creams and the giant jelly babies.

"Great! Some sugar should keep us going for a while," said Agatha, opening the jelly babies.

As we worked our way through the sweets and biscuits, we talked about school and our favourite subjects (English for me, geography for her). And we both agreed that maths was mostly pointless.

"You really find maths hard, don't you?" said Agatha.

I nodded.

"I thought you looked upset in class the other day."

It felt like a lifetime ago when I was trying not to cry in front of everyone.

"I just feel so useless in those classes," I said. "Mr Davy goes so fast when he explains stuff that I can't keep up. And I hate it when he fires questions at us on the spot."

Agatha ripped the head off a red jelly baby and grinned.

"Oh yeah, that's horrible when he does that! But he's really nice, Mr Davy, though, isn't he?"

I shrugged. "I guess."

I shoved a third custard cream into my mouth.

"You know what you should do. You should tell Mr Davy how worried you get about maths. He would probably help you a bit more if you did. Tell him he's going too fast."

I wasn't so sure about that. I couldn't tell a teacher what to do, could I?

Agatha put another jelly baby in her mouth.

"I did that with Ms Stapleton in French once. I told her I needed help to go over some things I didn't

244

understand and she was fine about it! And she's not even as nice as Mr Davy."

She was right. Ms Stapleton was well strict.

"I don't know. Maybe," I said.

Agatha looked back up at the night sky.

"Look! There's a plane. Where do you think it's heading?"

I watched the plane, its red light flashing as it flew across the dark sky.

"Cairo, I reckon," I said.

"Agreed!" said Agatha. "And there is a woman called Lucy, sitting in a window seat looking down on us right now. It's been her lifelong dream to go to Egypt to see the pyramids."

I looked up at the plane and waved.

"Hello, Lucy! Enjoy the pyramids!" I said.

Agatha laughed and we spent another hour spotting planes and making up destinations and people who were travelling on them. I came up with a man called Barry who was on his way to Australia to have surfing lessons, and Agatha said that on another plane there was a woman called Jane who was on her way to Antarctica to try and break the world record for building the world's biggest snowman. Agatha was rather good at this game.

I yawned and checked my watch.

"11.55. We're nearly there," I said, sipping on the last dregs of my cola. "What do you think is going to happen? At midnight? Will the date just change and we go home?"

Agatha shrugged. "I guess so." She belched. "I feel a bit sick, actually."

I knew what she meant. We'd eaten all of the biscuits and jelly babies.

"Me too," I said. I also felt really tired so maybe the sugar hadn't helped after all.

We flopped back on the grass just as a shooting star shot across the sky.

"Quick, make a wish!" said Agatha.

"I wish Monday would arrive," I said out loud.

Agatha closed her eyes and I guessed she was wishing for her mum's results to be OK. She checked her watch again.

"It's 11.59 and 50 seconds!" she said. "We've nearly made it to midnight, Cory. This is it! We're going back!"

We both sat up and the shock of the movement made my guts churn. I felt the biscuits, cola and jelly babies all mix up together in my stomach and I put my hand to my mouth.

"Cory? Are you all right?" said Agatha.

I shook my head, trying to keep the food inside my stomach.

"No," I said. "I think I'm going to be—"

CHAPTER
TWENTY-SEVEN

I opened my eyes and let out a little burp.

I blinked, looking around me. I wasn't outside any longer. I was in bed with a pillow under my head and a warm duvet over my body.

One second, I was at the top of Ivy Hill, about to vomit, and the next I was waking up in my bed. How did that happen?

I looked at my clock.

7.58 a.m.

And I could smell burning toast.

I closed my eyes and sighed.

After all that, we'd failed. I reached for my phone and messaged Agatha.

IT DIDN'T WORK!

I hit send. The smoke alarm began to beep and then Agatha replied.

Don't panic. We will try something else.

But I *was* panicking. We were stuck in an endless loop and I didn't understand what it was that we needed to do. I lay there, unmoving. Agatha sent another message.

Can you get out of going to your dad's awards today?

I tapped my reply.

Yes.

Meet me at the library at midday. There is an exhibition about Ivy Hill. I bet we'll find some answers there.

Of course! I remembered seeing a sign for it when I was tracing Agatha's movements that day. I was pleased we had something to try but I wasn't sure we'd find anything.

When Dad left for the awards, I quickly got ready and walked into town to meet Agatha. She was waiting for me by the library doors.

"Do you think we'll find anything useful?" I said.

"It's worth a try. Come on," said Agatha. Inside we followed the sign pointing to the Ivy Hill exhibition which led us into a large room. We were the only ones there. There was soft music playing and we looked at the displays along the wall. There were some coloured drawings of what our town might have looked like back in Ivy's day, an old map and a big photograph of Ivy Hill as it looks today. As we walked, we must have triggered a sensor as a woman's voice began to play through a hidden speaker.

The year is 1880 and Ivy Douglas is six years old. Boxwick is mostly farmland, and life for the villagers is governed by the success of their crops. Ivy's family are farmers and they work the local land...

The voice faded as we carried on, studying all the pictures and documents.

"I can't see how this is going to help," I said.

Agatha stopped by a glass cabinet.

"There's an old newspaper article in here," she said. "It's dated Sunday 15th October 1880. That's today's date!"

I went to take a closer look at the headline:

YOUNG GIRL SAVES TOWN FROM FIRE.

Agatha began to read the article. "She might be small, but six-year-old Ivy Douglas has a big heart when it comes to courage. Yesterday, when the farming town of Boxwick was dangerously close to being destroyed by a fierce field fire, the young child simply commanded the fire to 'go away' and the approaching flames retreated. 'My fellow townspeople and I were all witnesses to what I can only describe as a miracle,' said the town vicar Reverend Charles Godwin. 'Ivy Douglas saved our homes, our livelihoods and probably our lives.'

"When asked whether she was helped somehow by an outside influence, Ivy replied, 'No. I just wanted to put things right.'"

At the top of the article was a line drawing of a little girl standing on a hill, her arms outstretched towards a blazing field.

"Is there anything here about undoing the wish?" I said. I moved on to the other displays, feeling more and more desperate. "It's just stuff to do with history and what Ivy did. This isn't any use at all!"

Agatha scowled at me. "Calm down, Cory. We haven't looked at everything yet," she said.

But I didn't see the point. We weren't going to find anything.

Agatha got to the final display.

"There's an interview with Ivy as an adult!" said Agatha. "Come and see."

I wandered over. This article looked more recent than the other one, but it was still old and dated October 1950. Ivy was sitting in an armchair, an old lady now. She had a kind face. Her hands were folded in her lap and beside her, on a table, was a forest of framed photographs, mostly of people much younger than her. I guessed they were her family.

"It says here that Ivy did a lot for charity and raising money for local causes," said Agatha.

There was a small photo of Ivy standing in a bright children's ward in the local hospital. A sign above her head said it was called the Ivy Douglas Ward.

"Does she say anything about the hill?" I said, scanning the article.

"Yes!" said Agatha. "I'll read it. 'I know local people think that the hill has some kind of magical power, but on that day I was just a frightened child. I remember realizing that the adults around me were scared too. And that is a horrible feeling, isn't it? When you know the adults are worrying as well.'"

I knew how that felt. I hated seeing Mum and Dad worrying. Agatha continued reading.

"'I just wanted the fire to go away. And how do you do something like that when you're six? You just tell it to go away, of course. So that's what I did.'

"The interviewer in the article then asks what she thought about locals using the hill to make their own wishes. And Ivy replied, 'Who knows if the hill has magical powers or not? I was just trying to do the right thing that day and I've continued to live my life like that ever since. I think if we all tried to put things right a little, then the world would be a much nicer, kinder place, don't you think?'"

Agatha and I were silent.

"Put things right," I quoted. "Do you think there's something in that?"

Agatha frowned. "What do you mean?"

"I mean maybe we need to put the things that are wrong in this day, right. Like when I save that little boy's stuffed dragon from ending up in the pond."

"And when I stop that woman from walking into a lamp post!" said Agatha.

My heart began to race. We were on to something, I was certain of it! But surely it was an impossible task.

"But we can't put everything right in the whole world," I said. "Wars? Famine? The environment? What can we do about that?"

"We can play our part when we get back to normal, that's for sure," said Agatha. "But no, we can't solve things like that in a day. But Ivy said about people putting things right *a little*. It's like saying that the small things can still make a big difference." This was sounding more and more promising.

"What is there in your day that needs to be put right?"

Agatha began to list the things on her fingers.

"Let me see. So there's the woman who walks into the lamp post, a man knocks coffee over his friend, there's a boy on a bike who swerves around an old man who stumbles and drops all his shopping."

"I see him too!" I exclaimed. "He speeds through the park! I can stop that happening, I think. Anything else?"

"The hardest one is the puppy incident in the

market. It slips its collar and … well, it's utter mayhem. Put it that way. While the owner is chasing the dog she knocks over an artist's easel. Then a balloon seller loses all her balloons. It's chaos!"

That explained the bunch of balloons I'd seen in the sky when I'd been trailing Agatha.

"I've tried to help and catch the dog before it all kicks off, but it hasn't worked. How about you, Cory?"

I thought about my repeated day.

"You've seen the boy with the dragon, but I stop a jogger from skidding on a crisp packet, then I help a man to propose to his girlfriend."

"Really?" said Agatha.

"Yup! And that's about it, I think."

It didn't sound like much. I was confident I could put those things right.

"And what about at the awards thing you mentioned. Anything there?" said Agatha.

I thought about it.

"No. I don't think so. Unless you count my dad not winning of course!" I laughed, but then it dawned on me and everything fell into place.

"Of course!" I said. "Dad is supposed to win! His agent fixed things so that he doesn't."

"His own agent did that?" said Agatha.

"I know. Bad isn't it?"

Agatha nodded. "Yep. So that is another thing we'll need to put right then."

I frowned. "What, fix the awards so Dad wins?"

Agatha leaned forwards. "No, Cory. We *unfix* the awards so your dad wins. He's the true winner, right?"

"Yes."

"Well then. We need to correct a wrong to make a right. And Dennis Turner needs to hold that trophy."

I grinned when I thought about it. Dad actually winning? He'd be blown away!

We sat in the library for another half an hour, talking through our plans. I told Agatha my idea for how Dad could win the award and she got really excited when I told her that Johnnie Button was going to be there.

"He's so famous! Do you think I could meet him?"

I shrugged. "I guess so."

We worked through a few more details and then Agatha stood up.

"So we are going to try and put everything right tomorrow, yes?" I said. "I mean, tomorrow which is actually today, of course."

Agatha hesitated. I knew this was going to be hard for her – to leave this day and face whatever was going to happen on Monday. But then she took a deep breath and nodded.

"Yes. Tomorrow is the day we put things right and get back to normal," she said.

I grinned. "Let's do this."

CHAPTER
TWENTY-EIGHT

The next morning I woke up to the smell of burning toast, and a message from Agatha.

> All set? Dennis Turner is going to be a superstar tonight!

Butterflies fluttered around my stomach. I couldn't wait to see Dad's face when he won! He was the worthy winner. I sent a reply.

> Yep! Operation Get Back To Monday Morning is GO!

Agatha replied with a smiling-face emoji.

I got dressed and went down to the kitchen where the smoke alarm was beeping furiously as usual.

"Morning, Dad," I said, opening the back door. "I'll take Bingo out now, shall I?"

"That would be great, Cory," said Dad. "And when you get back you'd better have a shower and get ready. Exciting, isn't it?"

I smiled at him. "Yes, it is, Dad. I hope you win!"

Dad flushed as he concentrated on fanning the alarm. "Oh, I don't know about that. I'm just grateful to be nominated."

I checked the time on the oven. I had to get to the park a bit earlier and stop the boy stealing the woman's purse. It was going to be tight, but I had to put the first thing right.

"I've gotta go!" I said, running to the hallway. I stuffed my feet into my trainers, clipped Bingo's lead on and scooped him up under my arm.

"Bye, Dad! Wish me luck!" I hollered.

"Bye! Erm. Good luck?" said Dad. "Whatever that is for."

I heard my phone beep. It was the message from Mum. I wouldn't have time to reply to her today, but hopefully I'd be seeing her tomorrow!

I ran down the road, still carrying Bingo. If I let

him walk then we'd be too late. I hurried past the park entrance and down the road. Up ahead I could see the woman pushing the buggy as she talked on her phone. Behind her I could see the cyclist slowly sauntering along the road. He must have been looking out for opportunities to steal and it was only when he saw her open bag that he decided to strike.

I rushed down the hill. She was just a few metres from me now, but the cyclist was faster than I was and I saw him lean his head to one side, eyeing up her bag and the open zip.

I quickly waved my arm in the air.

"Hey! Excuse me!" I shouted. "Your bag is open!"

The woman looked up at me, but her expression was vague. She was clearly distracted by whoever was on the phone as she continued chatting.

I waved again.

"Quick!" I yelled. "Your bag!" The cyclist was just behind her now, his arm reaching forwards.

The woman frowned at me. Then, just as the cyclist was about to snatch the purse, she twisted the bag around to the front of her body and pulled on the zip. The cyclist swerved around her then bounced down the kerb and pedalled quickly down the road and past the park entrance. The woman was still on

260

her call, oblivious that she'd come so close to having her purse stolen.

"Excellent," I said, mentally ticking off number one. But I had to be speedy if I was going to solve number two. I ran back to the park entrance and saw the jogger three steps away from the crisp bag.

"STOP!" I shouted. The jogger came to an abrupt halt, her face full of alarm. I ran forward and picked up the rubbish.

"Sorry. You can carry on now," I said. She frowned at me and then carried on her way.

"Now for the snoggers," I said. I put Bingo down and he trotted along beside me until we got to the cafe.

Caroline and Wayne had already begun their argument.

"You have completely misunderstood me, yet again." said Wayne. I hurried over.

"Excuse me!" I said. "Sorry to interrupt but—" I knew this wasn't going to sound good but I had to hurry. "You see, the thing is. Wayne here has something he wants to ask you, Caroline. So it's really not worth having an argument right now."

"You what?" said Wayne. "What do you mean I've got something to ask her? She doesn't even like me right now!"

"But she does! Don't you, Caroline?" Caroline just shrugged and looked away.

"Look, I don't know what you think you're doing interfering with a private conversation, but could you just … go away?" said Wayne.

Oh no. This was going badly. Very badly. When it had worked previously, I had butted in before they'd begun to really argue. Had I left it too late this time?

I put on my best smile.

"OK. I'm going to leave you to it. But before I do, I just want to say something."

Wayne and Caroline were both staring at me. I swallowed.

"Well?" said Caroline.

"What I want to say is … you two are meant to be together. I see you in the park all the time and you are always so … happy! And you kiss a lot so that must mean you like each other, even if it is a bit icky."

Caroline smirked.

"Yes, you were about to have a bit of a row, but what really matters is how you feel about each other, isn't it? And Wayne really, really likes you, Caroline. I know because … because he's got something in his pocket that he was hoping to give to you today."

Wayne's mouth dropped open and Caroline looked at him.

"Have you, Wayne?"

In the distance I could hear the ducks quacking loudly and Bingo began to pull. I had to go.

"Just ask her, Wayne! Please!" I said. And then I picked Bingo up again and ran down towards the duck pond, hoping I wasn't too late.

I got to the pond and Archie had his arm stretched backwards, the soft dragon dangling down from his clutched fist. He threw it up, into the air.

"NO!" I shouted. I skidded along the dirt and jumped up, grabbing a thread of the dragon's tail with my fingertips. I'd done it!

"There you go," I said, handing the dragon to Archie. The woman and the old man were staring at me, open-mouthed.

"Can't hang around!" I said. I headed back to the path and was about to message Agatha when I heard a familiar voice.

"Well, if it isn't Mr *Déjà Vu* himself," said Will. "Waiting for us to see the damage you've caused, are you?"

I'd forgotten about Will and Rowan! Was this my chance of putting a wrong thing right? I couldn't keep running away from my problems. Besides. *I* had the upper hand in this situation. I knew *exactly* what they were going to say. I took a deep breath, then I did the opposite of what I felt like doing and stood right in front of them, placing Bingo down on the ground. He sniffed at the path.

"Hi, Will! Hi, Rowan! Off to watch the football, are you?" I said, brightly. I felt my heart pounding in my chest. I forced myself to stand a little taller.

Will looked confused by the tone of my voice. I was already behaving in a way he wasn't expecting, and it had unnerved him.

"Erm. Yeah," he said. "But I *nearly* couldn't go. Have you seen what you've done?" He gestured at the sling. He had a deep scowl on his face.

"Oh dear. Sorry about your arm," I said.

Will snorted. "Yes and you'd know all about that, wouldn't you? Considering it was you who got me into this situation in the first place!" He looked at Rowan to back him up, but Rowan was staring at the ground as usual.

"Well, if it was me then I've done you a bit of a favour then really, haven't I? Seeing as you hate swimming so much anyway. Gives you an excuse not to go, doesn't it?"

"What do you mean?" said Will. "I love swimming! In fact, I'm going to have to miss the county championships because of you!"

He jabbed a finger at me but, unfortunately for him, it was a finger from his arm that was in the sling. He clearly wasn't injured at all. Even Rowan looked surprised. Will realized what he'd done and then put on a false flinch as if he was now feeling how much it hurt.

"If you want to get out of swimming, don't make up lies. OK?" I said.

Will's eyebrows knotted together.

"What are you talking about? It's because of you I can't swim, so I'm not going to be winning any more trophies, am I?"

I sighed and took a step closer to him. "I've always been nice to you, Will. Maybe you could start doing the same to me for a change? And maybe talk to your dad? Tell him how you feel about swimming? I mean, what have you got to lose?"

Will stared at me, blinking.

"You'd better go to your football match now," I said. "I've got somewhere I need to be."

I stepped around them, turning back, one last time.

"They win 3–2, by the way," I said. Then I looked down at my little dog. "Come on, Bingo. Let's get home."

CHAPTER
TWENTY-NINE

Operation Park complete.

There was a pause as Agatha replied to my message.

Yay! See you soon for Puppy Mayhem!

I checked my watch. Time was running out.

This was not going to be easy.

I still had to make a new card declaring Dad as the true winner of the Best Daytime TV Game Show Presenter! All we had to do was to switch it with the one that Johnnie Button reads from. At the moment that felt near impossible but we had to try.

I had a shower, which took around five seconds,

then I got dressed and ran to my room.

I opened the drawer of my desk. It was crammed full of stuff and there was a plastic ruler jammed inside. I rattled and pulled it and eventually it sprang open. I found some old index cards that Mum had bought for me to make maths flashcards with, which I'd never done. I took the least creased one. I didn't have any envelopes, so I hurried downstairs to the kitchen to see what I could find there. Dad was outside, standing on the patio polishing his shoes. He hadn't seen me but I had to be quick. One drawer of our kitchen dresser was filled with random stuff like takeaway leaflets, batteries, tape measures and old phone chargers. I rummaged around and eventually found a yellowish envelope. OK, so it wasn't gold, but under the theatre lights it would probably look golden enough, wouldn't it? I grabbed a black felt-tip pen and I hurried to the lounge and knelt down at the coffee table. I placed the index card in front of me and began to write in my best handwriting.

AND THE WINNER IS ... DENNIS TURNER!

I put the card inside the envelope and sealed it. Then

I remembered that Johnnie had read the nominations from the back of the envelope. I tried to think back to what he had said. I remembered the other nominee was someone called Tabitha Jackson who presented *Old Dog, New Tricks*, then there was Dad and finally Timothy Gosling who presented *Your Cash, My Cash*.

I stuffed the envelope into the pocket of my trousers. I needed to hurry now to get to the market in time to help Agatha catch the dog. Dad was back in the kitchen.

"I've just got to go into town for something," I said.

"We haven't got time for that," said Dad. "We're leaving in ten minutes." He rubbed a cloth over his already shiny shoes.

"But it's important!"

Dad stopped what he was doing and looked at me.

"Is this some made-up story so that you can go to the football match?"

"No, Dad. I wouldn't do that! You know I wouldn't."

Dad didn't seem convinced.

"How about you pick me up by the library in fifteen minutes?" I said. "It's on the way."

Dad frowned. "I guess. But don't be late."

I turned to go and then stopped by Bingo's treat jar. I quickly opened it and took a meaty morsel – one of Bingo's favourite treats.

"What is it you're doing that's so urgent, anyway?" said Dad. "Surely it can wait?"

I headed down the hallway and turned to reply.

"I have to put something right!" I shouted and then I ran out of the door and sprinted down the road towards town.

I spotted Agatha standing by the town clock near the market. Just beyond her was a woman selling the brightly coloured balloons. I ran over to Agatha. There was no time to catch up.

"Where is it? Where's the puppy?" I asked, panting from all the running.

Agatha pointed to a young boy with a red-haired Labrador puppy bounding beside him. The puppy was wearing a pale blue collar with a long black lead. The boy was clearly struggling to keep him under control.

"That collar looks loose," I said. "Let's just go over and tell him and he can tighten it up. Easy!"

I started to walk towards him and Agatha followed.

"Excuse me?" I said. "I think your dog's collar is a bit—" But before I got a chance to finish my sentence the dog began to wriggle backwards, pulling its head and ears through the collar until it was free.

"Catch him!" said Agatha.

The boy tried to reach for the puppy but it was too fast.

"Monty! Stop!" he shouted.

The puppy bounded right in front of me and I held my arms out wide.

"You're a good doggy, aren't you?" I said. "Come on, just a little closer and—" I lurched forwards, but the puppy ducked away, thinking it was a game. Every direction I went in it jumped the opposite way, his large paws smacking against the pavement. Agatha scooted around to try and surprise him from the other side, but he swerved past her legs and was off.

"He's getting away!" said Agatha.

At the end of a row of stalls was an artist standing by a large canvas on an easel. The canvas was covered in colourful brushstrokes that captured the chaos of a Sunday market. The dog was heading straight towards it. Its tail wagging and its tongue dangling out of the side of his mouth. He was having such a good time!

I sprinted after Agatha and took the meaty morsel from my pocket and got ready to launch it into the air.

"Agatha! Catch!" I shouted.

The meaty morsel span on its arc towards Agatha. She jumped up, grabbing it in one hand. But the dog was about to crash straight into the painting. Agatha stopped and at the top of her lungs she yelled, "TREAT!"

The dog skidded to a halt and his head turned round. He sniffed the air and his ears pricked up and then he tentatively stepped towards Agatha, weighing up if the food was more enticing than having the chance to bound around. He crept closer and closer until Agatha gave him the treat and the boy grabbed Monty's shoulder and quickly put his collar back on – a little tighter this time.

"Yes! You did it!" I said.

"Thank you so much," said the boy who looked red and flustered. "That could have been an absolute disaster." We couldn't hang around. I turned to Agatha. "My Dad is going to pick us up outside the library. We need to be quick."

We pounded along the pavement and tried not to bump into anyone as we ran. I spotted Wayne and Caroline, standing by a flower seller who took a bright bunch of pink roses from a bucket and presented them to Caroline. She took them, then leaned towards Wayne and they began to kiss. I spotted a shiny diamond ring on her finger.

"Yes! Go Wayne!" I yelled, disturbing their kiss. Wayne grinned at me and waved. It had worked! Agatha was just ahead of me and she called back over her shoulder.

"Look! There's that boy!" The boy on the bike was being led along the road by a policeman. His head hung down. There was another policeman taking notes from a flustered looking man. It looked like the boy had been trying to steal again, but this time he'd been caught!

I sped up and ran beside Agatha as we swerved around a road sweeper.

"Does your dad know I'm coming with you?" Agatha gasped.

"No! I'll think of something. Don't worry," I said.

The welcome sight of the library was just up ahead and we sprinted the final few metres. There was a parking space right outside but it was empty.

We slowed down to a stop. I leaned my hands on to my knees as I caught my breath.

"Where … is … he?" I said, through gasps. If he was any longer we'd be too late to get to the theatre to make the switch.

"I don't think we're going to make it," I said to Agatha. But, just then, I heard a familiar popping sound and our car appeared around the corner and juddered to a halt in front of us.

"At last!" I said. I got in the front and Agatha dived into the back.

Dad looked round at Agatha.

"Oh, hello!" he said.

"This is Agatha, a friend from school," I said. "I'll explain when we're on the way. You don't want to be late, do you?"

Dad put the car into gear and it made a dreadful crunching noise.

"Right. Off we go!" he said.

I sat back in my seat and took a few long breaths.

So far we had managed to put all the wrongs right that had crossed our paths. There was just one more to resolve.

I'd discovered so much about my dad in these repeating twenty-four hours – the sacrifices he'd made for me and Mum, how insecure he was behind his loud personality *and* how loyal and trusting he was of his unscrupulous agent who was completely conning him.

It was imperative that Dad won that award. Or everything would have all been for nothing.

CHAPTER THIRTY

"Thank you for giving me a lift to the theatre, Mr Turner," said Agatha as we drove. "I bumped into Cory in town and he told me that you are up for an award. That's so exciting!"

"Why, thank you, Agatha! Yes, I must say I'm really looking forward to this. And where are you off to when we get there? Anywhere nice?"

There was a pause and for a moment I thought Agatha hadn't actually come up with a reason.

"I'm a fan of Johnnie Button. The DJ and influencer? And he's going to be there apparently. I'm going to see if I can get his autograph. And a selfie."

"Ah, never heard of him. But I'm sure he's a lovely chap," said Dad.

"Can you go a bit faster, Dad?" I said. "We don't want to be late."

I'd dreaded sitting through these awards so many times, but now I couldn't think of anywhere that I'd rather be in the whole world. The rest of my life depended on the outcome of the next few hours. It *had* to go well.

We got to the theatre car park and Dad swung the car into a space. I spotted Sydney talking to Timothy in the usual spot. And there, on the steps in his blazer and jeans, was Johnnie Button. We were just in time.

I took off my seat belt and jumped out of the car. Agatha did the same.

"Johnnie is over there," I said to her. I took the envelope out of my back pocket. "RUN!"

Agatha grabbed the envelope from my fingers and rushed across the car park. The woman with the clipboard was just handing Johnnie the original golden envelope. He took it and in three ... two ... one ... he dropped it, just as Agatha reached the bottom step.

"Ooh! Johnnie! Over here!" she called.

Johnnie turned his head and hesitated. This was the only opportunity we had to make the switch! He *had* to leave that envelope on the ground.

277

"Can I have a selfie, Johnnie?" called Agatha.

Johnnie was still half turned, a grin spread across his face.

"Of course you can!" he said. I thought Agatha had distracted him enough that he was going to leave the envelope for a moment, but then he snatched it up and put it into the right hand pocket of his blazer.

"Oh no!" I groaned.

Dad was now out of the car and he'd spotted his agent. "Sydney! Yoo-hooo! I'm over here!"

Agatha skipped up the steps to join Johnnie and she held her phone up in the air at arm's length. They both looked up at the screen with wide grins on their faces. Johnnie turned to her and said something and then he went inside.

Agatha trotted down the steps and came over to join me. She had a weird smirk on her face, but I couldn't see what was so amusing considering we'd failed.

"He is so cool," she said, flushing slightly.

"We didn't do it, Agatha. He's going to read out Timothy as the winner and we're going to be trapped in this day for ever."

I noticed that the envelope I'd made was missing from her hand.

"Where is it?" I said.

Agatha checked around to make sure no one was listening.

"I didn't manage to make the switch. But there is still a chance this could work," she said. The crowds were beginning to grow around us, and she took a step closer and spoke in a hushed voice. "When I took the selfie I put the envelope in his left pocket."

We still had hope after all!

"Do you remember which pocket he takes the envelope out of?"

I pictured the scene that I'd seen many times now. Did Johnnie reach into his right pocket for the envelope? Or was it the left?

"I'm not sure," I said. I thought hard. "He goes up to the microphone and pats at his pockets. Then he takes the envelope out of one of them. But I'm not sure which!"

"OK. We've just got to hope that he pats the left-hand pocket first and takes our one out," said Agatha.

"I guess," I said. This was so stressful and there was literally nothing we could do about it now. It was all down to chance.

"Cory? Are you coming?" Dad was near the main doors.

"I've got to go. I'll see you later."

Agatha smiled. "Good luck, Cory," she said.

I turned and made my way up the steps and into the theatre.

This was it. Everything boiled down to that envelope in Johnnie Button's pocket.

CHAPTER THIRTY-ONE

The ceremony happened just as before. Edward Wainwright appeared on stage and everyone still jumped when he coughed into the microphone. The speeches went on as before, but this time I was on the edge of my seat. As each award was presented I found myself gripping the arms of my chair. Before long we'd find out if Dad was going to be the true winner and if our plan had worked.

Then, after what felt like hours and hours of waiting, it was time.

"Now we move on to the Best Daytime TV Game Show Presenter," said Edward. "And here to read the nominations, I am delighted to welcome to the stage radio DJ, model, actor and influencer – Johnnie Button!"

Johnnie leapt out of his seat and skipped up the steps at the side of the stage.

"Hey, everyone! Nice to see you!" he boomed into the microphone.

This was it. This was the moment that could put everything right. Tomorrow I would wake up and it would be Monday. And I would get to see Mum again.

Johnnie's blonde hair shone under the bright spotlights.

"Right, so the three nominees for the Best Daytime TV Game Show Presenter award are... Oh, hang on a minute." I sat forward in my seat and crossed my fingers.

"Pick the left pocket, pick the left pocket," I whispered through gritted teeth.

Johnnie frowned, probably wondering why both pockets felt like they had something in them.

"Come on, Johnnie. Please pick the left," I said in a hushed voice.

Johnnie grinned out at the audience and then his hand reached down and he fumbled his fingers into the right-hand pocket, pulling out the shiny gold envelope.

"No," I said. I put my head in my hands. I felt Dad lean towards me.

"Everything all right, Cory?"

I didn't reply.

"I think I'll be needing this," said Johnnie over the microphone, and the audience laughed. I listened as he began to read. I couldn't believe it! Everything was over. I'd never see my mum again.

"So the nominees for Best Daytime TV Game Show Presenter are: Tabitha Jackson, from *Old Dog, New Tricks*…"

My ears began to ring and panic flooded my body. We'd failed. Agatha's little sister would never get older. *I'd* never get older! I'd never celebrate Christmas again or learn how to drive a car or travel further than a few hours from my home. He hadn't picked the right envelope and now we would be stuck here for ever. Johnnie's voice carried on in the background.

"Oh yeah! I remember this guy. So, the next nominee is Dennis Turner, presenter of the game show *Déjà Vu*."

Dad sat forward in his seat and waved his arm, just like before. It was so unfair. Dad was the winner – not Timothy!

"And finally, the presenter of *Your Cash, My Cash* … it's Timothy Gosling!"

Timothy stood up at the front and turned around. He was nodding at the crowd with a smarmy smile on his face. Sydney was grinning up at him, clapping her hands high in the air. I pressed my lips together. I had had enough of this.

Back on stage, Johnnie opened the envelope and pulled out a small white card as the applause for Timothy died down.

"And the winner is…" He took a dramatic pause.

Before I knew what I was doing, I shot up out of my seat and shouted at the top of my voice.

"STOP!"

There were gasps from the crowd and hundreds of heads turned around to face me. The photographer near the stage spun around and began to snap some pictures. I swallowed. What was I doing?

On stage, Johnnie was shielding his eyes from the bright spotlights, trying to see out into the audience.

"I'm sorry. What was that?" he said into the microphone.

I cleared my voice.

"I said stop!" I shouted. "This award is FIXED!"

There were more gasps from the crowd.

"Cory? What on earth are you doing?!" said Dad. He held on to my arm and tried to pull me back down.

"I'm putting something right, Dad," I said. "Don't worry. This is how it's supposed to be!"

I unfurled his fingers from my shirt and walked along our row and down the centre aisle. My heart was pounding in my chest.

"I'm not sure what is going on. Shall I read the card?" said Johnnie. He looked at the side of the stage to the organizers. Edward Wainwright was there, looking more pink than ever and the young assistant with the clipboard was standing beside him. No one said anything so Johnnie just shrugged.

"Well, OK then," he said. "I think we're going to see what this young guy has to say."

I headed to the steps and somehow managed to get up and on to the stage, even though my legs were trembling. The lights were dazzlingly bright, and I could hear the photographer taking photo after photo. I blinked as I approached the microphone. I had to stand on tiptoes to reach it.

"Um. Hello," I began. "My name is Cory."

The audience began to mutter again. I cleared my throat and they quietened down.

"The card that Johnnie has in his hand says that Timothy Gosling is the winner of the award," I said.

"YES!" said Timothy, leaping out of his seat and

punching the air. But no one applauded. They were too busy listening to me.

"But the thing is," I said. "The thing is that he isn't the true winner."

The crowd began to chatter and this time I spoke more loudly.

"The winner is my dad – Dennis Turner. But his agent, that woman there." I pointed at Sydney. "She wants Timothy to win because he's her new client and ... well, she thinks my dad is past it. So she paid that man there." I pointed to Edward. "To fix the vote. At least I'm pretty certain she paid him."

Edward opened and shut his mouth and looked outraged. There was an excited buzz in the theatre now as people discussed my revelation.

"I know you all think my dad is a bit of a joke," I said. "But it's not true. He is kind and talented. And he's a great dad. He deserves to win this award."

Johnnie laughed nervously.

"I'm not quite sure what to do here," he muttered, looking around at the officials. Suddenly the young woman with the clipboard, Edward's assistant, stepped forward and came to join me at the microphone. She gave me a kind smile and nodded for me to move to one side.

"Hello, everyone. My name is Aysha Barrett and I am the personal assistant to Edward Wainwright, the director of this event."

I noticed a few people shuffling forward in their seats. This was becoming gripping stuff.

"I have been working for Mr Wainwright for three long months now and the first thing I want to say is" – she turned to her boss – "I quit. You have been the worst person I have ever worked for and I can't bear to work with you for another second."

Edward shook his head and puffed his lips, like an angry ham-pink pony, then ducked behind the curtain, disappearing from view. Aysha smiled as she faced the crowd again, taking a deep breath. "Wow. That felt good," she said. There was some nervous laughter.

"And the second thing I want to say is that Cory here is speaking the truth. Sydney Court bribed Edward Wainwright to fix the award so that Timothy won. I wish I was as brave as this young man to have said something earlier. The real winner is sitting back there – in row V."

There was lots of fidgeting as everyone tried to strain their necks backwards to see. Suddenly Johnnie bounded back to the microphone.

"OK then. So it sounds like it's all sorted and, well, I've got somewhere to be … so it gives me great pleasure to announce that the winner of the Best Daytime TV Game Show Presenter is…" He looked at the card in his hand and ripped it into two.

"DENNIS TURNER!"

The crowd erupted into the loudest applause that I'd heard yet. Dad staggered to his feet, his mouth open. I grinned at him.

"You won, Dad! Come and get your trophy!" I said into the microphone.

He walked along the centre aisle and people began to stand and cheer! It was the most amazing thing I had ever seen. He came up on to the stage and the shiny discs on his suit shimmered and glinted under the lights. He shook Johnnie's hand and took the trophy. He stared at it, then held it beside him as he spoke into the microphone.

"Wow. Thank you so much!" said Dad. "That was so unexpected! I … um … I have a few people I'd like to thank…"

I spotted Sydney trying to calm Timothy, who was waving his hands around and looking very angry indeed. He eventually got up and stormed down the centre aisle and out of the door.

Sydney looked over at me, scowling, then grabbed her coat and bag and followed Timothy down the aisle. I had a feeling that would be the last that we'd be seeing of her.

I focused back on Dad.

"And, of course, I need to send my thanks to my fantastic son, Cory," said Dad. I could feel my cheeks burn red. I kept my eyes on Dad.

"Thank you, Cory. I know I embarrass you sometimes and that having me as a father isn't always the easiest thing. But" – he wiped a tear from his eye – "I wouldn't have won this award without you."

There was a collective "Ahhh" from the auditorium.

"I love you, son," continued Dad. "Thank you."

He waved the trophy in the air and the hall erupted into cheers and claps. I felt a lump forming in my throat. Crying was not part of the plan! I threw my arms around my dad, and he gave me the biggest hug back.

We'd done it.

CHAPTER THIRTY-TWO

On our way to Pizza Palace, I messaged Agatha.

DAD WON!

Agatha quickly replied.

I KNOW! It's all over social media!
What you did was amazing, Cory. You
were so brave!

When we got to the restaurant, Agatha rushed over
to the door to greet us.

"Congratulations, Mr Turner!" she said to Dad. "I
knew you could do it." She winked at me.

Dad hadn't stopped grinning, and he was still

clutching his award. "Thank you, Agatha. I can't believe it! Can you believe it?!"

Agatha grinned. "Yes, I can believe it! You won!"

Dad looked utterly stunned. He took a moment to let it all sink in. "I must ring your mum, Cory. She doesn't even know yet! But I think I'd better sit down to do this."

Dad went to the table where we usually ate and got his phone out. Tonight there'd be no phone call from Sydney asking him to open a block of toilets. Tonight was all about celebrating.

"How are you feeling, Cory?" said Agatha.

"Good, I think," I said. "But what if it's not enough? What if tomorrow is just today again?"

Agatha took a breath. "Who knows what tomorrow is going to bring?" she said. "Just enjoy every single second of 'right now'." She looked behind her at her family. "That's exactly what I'm going to do."

She turned back to me. "Right, I'd better go back. Let's think positive. I will see you at school tomorrow morning. Is that a deal, Cory?"

She held out her hand.

I smiled. I wasn't convinced she was right, but the alternative was too worrying to think about. Like she said, I'd concentrate on the "right now". "Yes, Agatha.

I will see you at school tomorrow." I said, and we shook hands.

She grinned and then headed back to her sister and dad.

I sat down with Dad and caught the end of his conversation with Mum. I could hear her screaming with joy at the other end.

"Yes … yes, he's here. Hang on. I'll pass you over." He held the phone towards me. "Your mum wants a word."

I took the phone and put it to my ear.

"Hello?"

"CORY! Oh my goodness, can you believe it? Your dad has told me everything you did. You are amazing, do you know that?"

Hearing her voice made me well up. I found it hard to speak.

"Uh-huh," I said.

"We are going to have to celebrate when I get back tomorrow. I can't wait to see you, Cory."

"I can't wait to see you too, Mum." I quickly passed the phone back to Dad before I started to cry.

Dad said bye to Mum and then he put the phone down, placing his hands flat on to the table.

"Right. Everything is going to be different from

now, Cory. Because of this award the offers of work will start coming in – and I mean proper, serious work. No more being paid in toothpaste! We can get the car fixed at last! Maybe we could spend a bit on updating the house a little. And then you can be proud of your old dad."

He gave me a small smile. I felt terrible.

"I am proud of you, Dad," I said. "I've just not been very good at showing it. That's all."

Dad leaned back in his seat. "It can't be easy having a parent in the spotlight. A faded spotlight at that!"

I wanted to talk to him again about finding a new agent and pursuing an acting career. But that could wait for now.

He picked up the trophy and gave it a little kiss before putting it back down again.

"Right, shall we order?" said Dad. He picked up a menu from the table. "We haven't had pizza in ages, have we? What a treat."

I laughed to myself. "Yes, it's lovely," I said. And I looked down at the menu that I now knew backwards.

That night I got my school bag ready and laid my uniform over the back of my chair. My phone beeped as the onslaught of messages on the school group chat began. I braced myself to read them again, but when I swiped the screen there wasn't anything from Will. Instead there was a flurry of messages about Dad's win.

Did you see Cory's dad won a TV award?!

Oh what?! No!

Yeah, I saw that. How amazing! My nan loves that show.

His dad is going to be well famous now.

The stream continued. Some were predicting that Dad might become a film actor and others said that he could be approached for some sponsorship deals that could be worth lots of money. I read them all and didn't say anything. Will's name popped up at the end and I prepared myself to read something horrible.

That's cool. Well done, Dennis.

I was gobsmacked! Will had said something nice? About my dad? Well, that was a first. Maybe my comments in the park had had an effect?

I turned my phone off and lay back, staring at the ceiling. If this was the final repeat of Sunday then it would be the perfect one to end on. Everything felt like it had fallen into place. I closed my eyes and whispered to myself.

"Please work," I said. "Please let it be Monday tomorrow."

There was nothing more I could do. We'd tried our best and all I could do now was to wait and see what the morning would bring. I rolled over, closed my eyes and drifted off to sleep.

CHAPTER
THIRTY-THREE

I woke to the sound of beeping.

I took a deep breath and screwed my eyes tightly shut. It was the smoke alarm. Dad's burnt toast had triggered it and I was here again. Stuck.

But then my eyes flashed open, widely.

That beeping sounded different. It wasn't the smoke alarm.

It was my alarm clock!

I sat up and grabbed it, slapping it on the top to stop the beeping.

7.30 a.m.

Not 7.58 a.m.

But 7.30 a.m.

I sniffed the air.

Nothing. I couldn't smell a thing.

I picked up my phone and turned it on. I looked over at my school backpack. It was packed! My uniform was lying over my chair, just how I'd left it last night.

My phone lit up and the screen filled with a photo of Bingo with his tongue sticking out.

The time read:

7.31 a.m.

And then beneath it was the date.

Monday, 16th October

"YES!" I shouted. "WE DID IT!"

A message flashed up on the screen.

IT'S MONDAY!!!

It was from Agatha. I quickly replied.

I KNOW!!!

I jumped out of bed and ran downstairs. Dad was filling up the dishwasher with the radio blaring in the background.

"DAD!" I shouted. "You're filling the dishwasher!"

Dad turned around. I must have looked a sight as I stood there with a massive grin on my face. I was never usually this happy on a Monday morning.

"Um, yes. I am," said Dad.

"And you've got the radio on too! You never have the radio on! You're usually waving a tea towel at the smoke alarm! This is BRILLIANT!"

Dad stood holding a dirty plate, staring at me.

"Are you feeling OK, Cory?" said Dad.

I hurtled myself across the kitchen and threw my arms around him.

"I'm fine. I'm absolutely fine," I said. Dad froze for a moment, then tightened his grip around me, stroking my hair. Behind him I spotted the trophy from last night, sitting on the kitchen counter. He was still the winner! I squeezed him even harder.

"You won the award, Dad! You did it!"

Dad let me go. "I still can't quite believe it," he said. Then he ruffled my hair and went back to the dishwasher.

"Oh, and I've fired Sydney," said Dad. "I'm

meeting an agent for lunch today to chat about my career and which direction it might go in. She really listened to me when I said I wanted to get back into acting and she even mentioned a couple of auditions that are coming up. What do you think about that?"

"Yes! That's brilliant, Dad." I said.

"It's scary! But it's exciting too." He straightened up and put a hand on his chest. "You know, I haven't felt this excited about work in a long while, I can tell you. I was just going through the motions before. But this? Well, this feels real. And your mum is excited too. She's at the airport now on her way home."

Dad closed the dishwasher and turned it on.

My phone beeped in my hand and I almost choked when I saw the message.

Hi Darling! I'm just boarding the plane now. I can't wait to see you! Mum x

It was Mum! She was coming home and I was going to see her! This day was just getting better and better. I replied.

YAY!

I made myself a bowl of cereal and sat at our kitchen table. Bingo had spotted I was in the kitchen and made his way towards me, his toenails clicking on the tiled floor and his tail wagging.

"Hello, Bingo," I said, scratching his ear. "You're the best dog, aren't you? Such a good dog."

Bingo licked his lips and then wandered over to his bed, flopping down for another sleep. He was another day older, which made me feel a little sad. I wondered how Agatha was doing. Her mum's hospital appointment was this morning. I imagined there would be a lot of worry in her house right now.

I finished getting ready, then I yelled goodbye to Dad and headed off to school. My stomach churned as I walked. It felt a bit like I'd been on a really long holiday and this was my first day back.

I got to school and just seeing the building was enough to make my insides clench. I'd had a life-changing experience but it hadn't stopped me from worrying. Will was probably in the school office right now, telling them lies about how I'd hurt his arm. And then there was Rowan who was probably not going to be mates with me any more. But for a change I didn't feel too bothered about that.

I walked through the school gates, amazed to see

everyone there just carrying on like it was a normal Monday morning.

"Hi, stranger!"

I spun around.

"Agatha! You're here!" I said.

"It's weird, isn't it?" said Agatha. "I feel like I've been in a dream or something."

She was smiling but her forehead was creased and her eyes looked a bit red.

"When will you hear about your mum?"

"Not until after school. But we're trying to think positively about it all."

"I'm sure it'll be OK," I said, and Agatha smiled. But then I worried that I shouldn't have said that in case it wasn't all OK. I had no idea what you were supposed to say in situations like this, but Agatha didn't seem upset with me.

We began to walk towards the main doors when I heard a familiar shout coming from behind me.

"Now *that's* déjà vu!"

I slowly turned around.

It was Will. OK, so he was using the same annoying catchphrase, but he didn't have his arm in a sling. Was he not going to report me to the office after all?

"You all right?" said Will. I looked at Agatha who

seemed as puzzled as I was. Will was talking to me? Asking if I was all right?

"Um. Yeah," I said.

Will nodded but didn't say anything. It was a bit awkward, the three of us standing there in silence, but then he cleared his throat.

"I spoke to my dad last night," he mumbled. "About what you said in the park. About not wanting to do swimming any more. You were right about that actually."

"Oh. Was it OK?" I said.

Will shrugged. "Yeah. He was a bit angry and stuff. But when he calmed down he said he understood. I really like cycling so we're going to start going out together once a week. So that's good, I guess. And no more training." He glanced up at me and grinned and I could see the relief in his face.

"Good. I'm glad you sorted it out," I said.

"Yeah. See you later," he said. Then he pulled his backpack a bit higher on to his shoulder and walked off.

I looked at Agatha, her eyes wide. "What was all that about?" she said.

"It was just something I said yesterday in the park."

"Right. I'd better get to form," said Agatha. "Catch you later."

She hurried off and I walked along the path to the main doors and spotted Rowan up ahead. We were in the same form so we fell in line, slowly walking together.

"All right?" he said. I nodded. "Look, Cory. I've been thinking since I saw you in the park yesterday. I'm sorry I went off with Will."

"Forget it," I said.

Rowan smiled. "Oh good. I thought you were going to be really angry with me!"

I shrugged. It didn't matter any more.

Rowan elbowed me. "Hey, do you want to come to the victory parade with us next weekend? I'm sure Will won't mind."

Normally I would have jumped at going for fear of being left out or losing my friend. But now I actually didn't want to go.

"Thanks, but you should just go with Will," I said.

Rowan frowned and then he nodded.

"Sure, OK," he said.

In form I sat in my usual seat and felt a sense of panic when I remembered what my next lesson was. Maths. I had relived the same day over and over and still hadn't managed to do any revision. It was going to be a disaster.

But the exam was nowhere near as bad as I had

expected. I surprised myself by answering more questions than I thought I would. I left a lot blank, but at least I'd given it a shot.

At the end of the exam, Mr Davy came around and collected the test sheets and the bell went for the next lesson. I remembered what Agatha had said, about asking for help when you needed it, so I walked to the front of the class where Mr Davy was sitting, busy putting all the papers into a folder. He glanced up.

"Cory! How can I help you?" he said.

"I … erm … I am kind of struggling a bit. With maths," I said.

Mr Davy nodded and sat back in his seat.

"I know. I see the panic in your face sometimes," he said. "What would you like me to do to help?"

I hadn't thought about that part. Mr Davy sat forward and rested his arms on his desk.

"How about we meet up one lunchtime this week and go over a few things?" he said. "It might be something a few of the other students would like to do too. We can cover anything that you're finding tricky. How does that sound?"

My face spread into a grin. "That sounds great," I said. I couldn't believe I was happy to be doing extra maths. "Thanks, sir."

*

After school I spotted Agatha walking ahead in a throng of people. I swerved around everyone to join her.

"Hi!" I said brightly. "Do you fancy going out at the weekend? Definitely no pizza though."

Agatha laughed. "*Definitely* no pizza." She smiled. "Yes, maybe. But can we see how things are first?"

"Of course," I said. If the news about her mum wasn't good I doubted she'd be in the mood for going out.

"Has your day been all right?" she asked.

I nodded. "It's been pretty good, actually! I talked to Mr Davy about maths and he's going to give me some extra lessons so thanks for that."

"That's great!" said Agatha. She seemed happy, but I could tell she was distracted. I guess she was worried about what news she'd be facing when she got home.

We came to a junction where Agatha had to go in a different direction and she turned to face me.

"I really hope everything is OK, Agatha."

She nodded and attempted a smile.

"Thanks, Cory. I'll see you tomorrow,' she said, and then she turned and hurried down the road towards home.

CHAPTER THIRTY-FOUR

When I saw our house I began to run. There was someone at home who I really, *really* wanted to see.

Mum opened the front door as soon as I reached our gate.

"Hi, Cory!" she said.

I ran towards her and threw my arms around her. She hugged me back and kissed me on the top of my head.

"Oh, that's a lovely welcome," she said. "Did you have a good weekend? Dad has been telling me all about it."

I squeezed my arms tightly. It felt so long since I'd seen her, I didn't want to let go.

"Cory, are you OK?"

"I'm fine. I'm just really pleased to see you. It's

been so long," I said, my voice muffled against her jumper. Eventually, I loosened my grip and Mum got a chance to look at me closely.

"It's only been a week. Oh, are you crying, darling?" she said, wiping my cheek. "Come on. Let's get you indoors."

I stepped into the house and suddenly the emotion of everything hit me.

"Cory, what on earth is wrong?" Mum said. She took my hand and led me to the lounge and we sat on the sofa. "Now, what are all these tears for? Has something happened?"

I didn't know where to start. *So* much had happened and it suddenly all felt incredibly overwhelming: seeing my dad being conned by Sydney, Will telling his lies about me, worrying I'd never see Mum again, Agatha worrying about her mum's illness.

"What is it, Cory? I've not seen you cry like this in years."

I took a deep breath. Bingo wandered over to me, his tail wagging. He'd only just realized I was home. When he was younger, he used to run to the door when I came in. He suddenly looked really old and he seemed to be a little unsteady on his legs. Had he always been like that? I bent down and gave him a rub around his ears. There was no way I could explain everything that had happened to Mum. It was all completely unbelievable. But I thought I knew how I could say it in another way.

"I don't ... I don't want Bingo ... to die," I said. "He's getting old and I want him to be with us for ever."

I felt like I was six again. This was awful.

"Oh, Cory. I'm so sorry," said Mum. "I know, it's a horrible feeling when you worry about losing a pet. But Bingo is fine at the moment, OK? He's getting old, yes. But he's healthy and he's probably got a lot of life in him yet."

I nodded, wiping at my nose. "Do you really think so?"

Mum got up and passed me a tissue.

"We can't stop time, Cory. There will be a day when, yes, Bingo won't be with us any more."

A little sob escaped my mouth.

"But I *could* stop time. I could have kept the day going over and over and Bingo would have lived for ever. We all would have!"

Mum put her hands on my face.

"What are you talking about, Cory?" she said. I could see that she was worried hearing me say something so strange.

I took a breath.

"It's nothing," I said. "It was just … a dream. I had a dream last night that I was stuck in the same day over and over and, even though it was horrible, it had good parts to it as well. Like everyone living for ever. But then you weren't here so that wasn't nice."

Mum put an arm around me and I leaned my head on her shoulder.

"If you think about it, your dream sounds a bit dull," she said. "How boring would life be if the same thing happened day in and day out. That wouldn't be very exciting, would it?"

"No. It's not," I said. I knew that from experience. "We have to keep moving forwards or we'd never get anywhere."

There was something else worrying me. Something that I hadn't ever said out loud before – an underlying fear I'd had for a while now.

"But what about you and Dad," I said. "What if you keep moving forward, and then … then you realize you don't want to be together any more."

Mum looked stunned. "Cory? Where has all this come from?" she said.

I stared down at my knees. "You seem to get annoyed with Dad all the time. I know he can be

309

embarrassing sometimes but … but I don't want you to split up."

"What? We're not splitting up, Cory," said Mum. "I just get frustrated with your dad sometimes. I don't think he realizes how talented he is! But now that he's got rid of that awful Sydney, I think things are about to change."

"Are you sure?" I said, sniffing.

She sighed. "There're always ups and downs in a relationship, Cory. I can't promise you that we won't argue on occasion or get fed up with each other. That's just how it is for most couples. But when I was away, I missed your dad as much as I missed you. And I'm so excited that he's decided to make some changes in his career. It's been a long time coming."

She gave me a kiss, then got up.

"Right. I'll make some tea and you go and get changed. We are going out tonight to celebrate your dad's award! I thought we'd give that new burger place a try?"

"OK," I said, relieved it wasn't Pizza Palace again. Before she went I gave her another quick hug and she stroked the top of my head. It was nice to have Mum home.

I went up to my room and put my school blazer on to the back of my chair, then packed my school bag ready for Tuesday. Time was moving on now and there wasn't anything I could do about it. Soon it would be the weekend, and before I knew it Christmas would be upon us, and then we'd be welcoming in a brand-new year. Everything was constantly changing and moving forwards and, although it was sometimes scary, I knew that this was exactly as it should be.

CHAPTER THIRTY-FIVE

Bingo's front right paw was digging into my thigh and I lifted him up and repositioned him a little. I looked down the row at Agatha's dad who had Maggie asleep on his lap. Her head was thrown back on his shoulder and she was dribbling from her open mouth on to his shirt. I giggled. Having a toddler on your lap looked far more awkward than a Jack Russell.

"It was so nice of the theatre to let you bring Bingo in," said Agatha. She reached towards Bingo and straightened the gold bow tie that Mum had attached to the back of his collar. This was a very special occasion so Bingo needed to look his best. He lifted his head towards Agatha and, for a moment, he looked like he was smiling.

Mum was on my other side and she leaned forward.

"The director said it would be fine as it's only preview night. Although I must admit, I wasn't expecting it to be this busy." It was only a small theatre but it looked like every seat was taken. Mum flicked through the programme a couple of times, then began to tap it on her knee. I pressed my hand to stop her tapping.

"He's going to be fine, Mum. Stop worrying."

Mum pressed her lips into a smile, then began to tap the programme again.

Agatha's mum reached a bag of sweets across Agatha and towards us.

"Humbug, Cory? Jenna?"

We both took one. Agatha's mum was looking better every time I saw her. Her light brown hair was a few inches long now and Agatha said she didn't need to go back to the hospital for a while. Everything was going well.

"Can I have a look at that?" I said to Mum. She passed me the programme and I turned to the cast list. The first actor was Dad who was playing the inspector. There was a black and white photograph of him and a paragraph about his TV work and how he was now returning to his first love – theatre acting.

"I'm so proud of him but I'm really nervous," whispered Mum. "I've got butterflies!"

I closed the programme and passed it back to her.

"Dad has got this, you know he has. Look at how much he's been rehearsing over the past few weeks. I think even Bingo knows his lines!"

Bingo let out a snort and Mum smiled and squeezed my arm. Just then the lights began to dim. Agatha made a quite little squeal and shuffled in her seat.

"Here we go," said Mum, quietly. "Come on, Dennis. You can do it."

I grinned to myself in the darkness as the thick, heavy curtain began to rise.

Dad was going to be brilliant. I just knew it.